ENGLISH TEXTS

Edited by
Theo Stemmler

4

Augustan Poetry

Edited by Gerd Stratmann

MAX NIEMEYER VERLAG TÜBINGEN

1970

The purpose of this series is to provide students and teachers of English with reliable editions of texts from all periods of English literature, language and culture. Each volume contains a representative selection of typical texts and will enable students and teachers to discuss the most important questions arising in university classes on these subjects. Comprehensive bibliographies will facilitate further research.

ISBN 3 484 44003 1

© Max Niemeyer Verlag Tübingen 1970
Alle Rechte vorbehalten. Printed in Germany
Satz: Karl Schenk Reutlingen-Sondelfingen
Druck: Karl Grammlich Pliezhausen
Einband von Heinr. Koch Tübingen

CONTENTS

V

VI. Memorial Verse

VII. Hymns

PREFACE

Eighteenth-century English poetry is no longer, as the habitually echoed complaints would make us believe, coldly neglected or underrated by modern scholarship. But while the interest in Pope and his contemporaries is steadily growing, its motives seem to have changed in a significant manner. The formal perfection and delicate balance of a poem like *The Rape of the Lock* remain undisputed and are still appreciated as such; there is, however, a strong tendency among students and younger scholars to understand these aesthetic qualities more and more in terms of their social and cultural function, i. e. in historical terms rather than as an embodiment of "timeless" human values and attitudes. The following selection of "Augustan" poetry, intended mainly for the hands of the student, has tried to do justice to this specific interest.

The title has been chosen, for the sake of convenience, to signify the poetry of the four decades between Queen Anne's accession (1702) and the end of Walpole's government (1742). Most historians would agree that this is as near as one could get, if attempting to "fix" the limits of one of the crucial stages in English social and literary history. The term "Augustan" does not, however, imply the exclusion of "low" kinds of poetry or, for that matter, of any kind at all. In principle, any poem written in the period just defined was eligible, including poems by authors whose main works belonged either to an earlier or to a later period (Congreve, Johnson).

This indicates already that the editor has deviated slightly from the course of well-balanced compromise taken by most anthologists. His main purpose was not to offer a fastidious choice of poetic gems or to present a few outstanding personalities. Instead, he has concentrated on the historical and, in a sense, impersonal context of Augustan poetry, which certainly includes the low poetry of the time (as Swift's poems illustrate) and was itself, as a whole, a dynamic element within the greater context of eighteenth-century English civilization. Thus poems of "public" relevance, standing not too far from the cultural centre of gravity and exemplifying important social roles of Augustan art, have been preferred to anthology pieces which might represent their author's personal idiom more happily or have a more immediate appeal to modern taste, but are of a rather "private" character.

The Augustan obsession with form and genre, and with the art of "correct" but at the same time "natural" imitation, is one of the most conspicuous features of the period. It revealed itself as a desperate attempt to force the disintegrating elements of aristocratic culture back into the harmony of a borrowed ideal. On the other hand, "mock"-versions and parodies of practically all the traditional genres by far outnumbered the "straight" poems, — a fact which demonstrates a remarkable artistic sincerity. It was mainly the novel and to a lesser degree the drama and the essay which attempted the intellectual and emotional assessment of the *new* society just emerging. The part acted by most of the poets was quite different, though hardly less important: they tested, as it were, the vitality of the ideals which the *old* elite claimed to represent. Unless writing in defiance of the realities of their time, they exposed a credibility gap not to be bridged by any formal effort. Their satires, parodies, mixtures of high and low forms, "unified" by the principle of incongruence itself, could but confirm the gap. In the end, these works probably contributed to the replacement of the old social order as effectively as Defoe's or Richardson's novels.

The foregoing general considerations led to the grouping of the poems according to genre instead of author. It is hoped that this arrangement will be especially welcomed by the student, to whom it offers some important lines of orientation, directing his attention almost immediately to certain connections, parallels, and contrasts. These advantages seem to outweigh the possible objection that work in seminars might be predetermined by such an arrangement.

Nearly all the groups of poems contain some typical "mock"-versions, which have proved to be of great didactic help in any introduction to conventions of Augustan poetry. Apart from simplifying the main patterns of the originals and thereby making them more transparent, they usually expose the moral concepts and social applications tacitly implied in the conventions.

The only extract reprinted here is the first part of the *Essay on Criticism,* a poem too important and influential to be simply omitted, but so long and, in parts II and III, so intricate that the compromise of an extract appeared to be both necessary and tolerable. The editor is aware that the assignment of some of the poems to a particular genre is but provisional and that his decisions are in several cases open to debate.

As far as the text is concerned, the idea of reprinting first editions only was discarded after some hesitation. While it seemed to accord best with the principles stated above, there was, on the other hand, the understandable interest of students and readers in owning the "best" text. This finally decided the issue: where there is a scholarly edition, that text has been followed (see 'Textual Sources' and 'Bibliography').

Erlangen   G. St.

I. ARS POETICA

Alexander Pope

AN ESSAY ON CRITICISM

[Part I]¹

'TIS hard to say, if greater Want of Skill
Appear in *Writing* or in *Judging* ill;
But, of the two, less dang'rous is th'Offence,
To tire our *Patience,* than mis-lead our *Sense:*
5   Some few in *that,* but Numbers err in *this,*
Ten Censure wrong for one who Writes amiss;
A *Fool* might once *himself* alone expose,
Now *One* in *Verse* makes many more in *Prose.*
    'Tis with our *Judgments* as our *Watches,* none
10 Go just *alike,* yet each believes his own.
In *Poets* as true *Genius* is but rare,
True *Taste* as seldom is the *Critick*'s Share;
Both must alike from Heav'n derive their Light,
These *born* to Judge, as well as those to Write.
15 Let such teach others who themselves excell,
And *censure freely* who have *written well.*
Authors are partial to their *Wit,* 'tis true,
But are not *Criticks* to their *Judgment* too?
    Yet if we look more closely, we shall find
20 Most have the *Seeds* of Judgment in their Mind;
Nature affords at least a *glimm'ring Light;*
The *Lines,* tho'touch'd but faintly, are drawn right.
But as the slightest Sketch, if justly trac'd,

1 [As to the division of the *Essay* "into three principal *parts* or members",
cf. *Twickenham Edition,* I, 237-38, and 239n.]

Is by ill *Colouring* but the more disgrac'd,
25 So by *false Learning* is *good Sense* defac'd;
Some are bewilder'd in the Maze of Schools,
And some made *Coxcombs* Nature meant but *Fools*.
In search of *Wit* these lose their *common Sense*,
And then turn Criticks in their own Defence.
30 Each burns alike, who can, or cannot write,
Or with a *Rival*'s, or an *Eunuch*'s spite.
All *Fools* have still an Itching to deride,
And fain *wou'd* be upon the *Laughing Side*:
If *Mævius* Scribble in *Apollo*'s spight,
35 There are, who *judge* still *worse* than he can *write*.
    Some have at first for *Wits*, then *Poets* past,
Turn'd *Criticks* next, and prov'd plain *Fools* at last;
Some neither can for *Wits* nor *Criticks* pass,
As heavy Mules are neither *Horse* nor *Ass*.
40 Those half-learn'd Witlings, num'rous in our Isle,
As half-form'd Insects on the Banks of *Nile;*
Unfinish'd Things, one knows not what to call,
Their Generation's so *equivocal:*
To tell'em, wou'd a *hundred Tongues* require,
45 Or *one vain Wit's,* that might a hundred tire.
    But *you* who seek to *give* and *merit* Fame,
And justly bear a Critick's noble Name,
Be sure *your self* and your own *Reach* to know,
How far your *Genius, Taste,* and *Learning* go;
50 Launch not beyond your Depth, but be discreet,
And mark *that Point* where Sense and Dulness *meet*.
    Nature to all things fix'd the Limits fit,
And wisely curb'd proud Man's pretending Wit:
As on the *Land* while *here* the *Ocean* gains,
55 In *other Parts* it leaves wide sandy Plains;
Thus in the *Soul* while *Memory* prevails,
The solid Pow'r of *Understanding* fails;
Where Beams of warm *Imagination* play,
The *Memory*'s soft Figures melt away.
60 One *Science* only will one *Genius* fit;

So *vast* is Art, so *narrow* Human Wit:
Not only bounded to *peculiar Arts,*
But oft in *those,* confin'd to *single Parts.*
Like Kings we lose the Conquests gain'd before,
65 By vain Ambition still to make them more:
Each might his *sev'ral Province* well command,
Wou'd all but *stoop* to what they *understand.*
    First follow NATURE, and your Judgment frame
By her just Standard, which is still the same:
70 *Unerring Nature,* still divinely bright,
One *clear, unchang'd,* and *Universal* Light,
Life, Force, and Beauty, must to all impart,
At once the *Source,* and *End,* and *Test* of *Art.*
Art from that Fund each *just Supply* provides,
75 Works *without Show,* and *without Pomp* presides:
In some fair Body thus th'informing Soul
With Spirits feeds, with Vigour fills the whole,
Each Motion guides, and ev'ry Nerve sustains;
It self unseen, but in th'*Effects,* remains.
80 Some, to whom Heav'n in Wit has been profuse,
Want as much more, to turn it to its use;
For *Wit* and *Judgment* often are at strife,
Tho' meant each other's Aid, like *Man* and *Wife.*
'Tis more to *guide* than *spur* the Muse's Steed;
85 Restrain his Fury, than provoke his Speed;
The winged Courser, like a gen'rous Horse,
Shows most true Mettle when you *check* his Course.
    Those RULES of old *discover'd,* not *devis'd,*
Are *Nature* still, but *Nature Methodiz'd;*
90 *Nature,* like *Liberty,* is but restrain'd
By the same Laws which first *herself* ordain'd.
    Hear how learn'd *Greece* her useful Rules indites,
When to repress, and when indulge our Flights:
High on *Parnassus'* Top her Sons she show'd,
95 And pointed out those arduous Paths they trod,
Held from afar, aloft, th'Immortal Prize,
And urg'd the rest by equal Steps to rise;

Just *Precepts* thus from great *Examples* giv'n,
She drew from *them* what they deriv'd from *Heav'n.*
100 The gen'rous Critick *fann'd* the *Poet's Fire,*
And taught the World, *with Reason* to *Admire.*
Then Criticism the Muse's Handmaid prov'd,
To dress her Charms, and make her more belov'd;
But following Wits from that Intention stray'd;
105 Who cou'd not win the Mistress, woo'd the Maid;
Against the Poets *their own Arms* they turn'd,
Sure to hate most the Men from whom they *learn'd.*
So modern *Pothecaries,* taught the Art
By *Doctor's Bills* to play the *Doctor's Part,*
110 Bold in the Practice of *mistaken Rules,*
Prescribe, apply, and call their *Masters Fools.*
Some on the Leaves of ancient Authors prey,
Nor Time nor Moths e'er spoil'd so much as they:
Some dryly plain, without Invention's Aid,
115 Write dull *Receits* how Poems may be made:
These leave the Sense, their Learning to display,
And those explain the Meaning quite away.
    You then whose Judgment the right Course wou'd steer,
Know well each ANCIENT's proper *Character,*
120 His *Fable, Subject, Scope* in ev'ry Page,
Religion, Country, Genius of his *Age*:
Without all these at once before your Eyes,
Cavil you may, but never *Criticize.*
Be *Homer's* Works your *Study,* and *Delight,*
125 Read them by Day, and meditate by Night,
Thence form your Judgment, thence your Maxims bring,
And trace the Muses *upward* to their *Spring;*
Still with *It self compar'd,* his *Text* peruse;
And let your *Comment* be the *Mantuan Muse.*
130   When first young *Maro* in his boundless Mind
A Work t'outlast Immortal *Rome* design'd,
Perhaps he seem'd *above* the Critick's Law,
And but from *Nature's Fountains* scorn'd to draw:
But when t'examine ev'ry Part he came,

4

135 *Nature* and *Homer* were, he found, the *same*:
Convinc'd, amaz'd, he checks the bold Design,
And Rules as strict his labour'd Work confine,
As if the *Stagyrite* o'erlook'd each Line.
Learn hence for Ancient *Rules* a just Esteem;
140 To copy *Nature* is to copy *Them.*
    Some Beauties yet, no Precepts can declare,
For there's a *Happiness* as well as *Care.*
Musick resembles *Poetry,* in each
Are *nameless Graces* which no Methods teach,
145 And which a *Master-Hand* alone can reach.
If, where the *Rules* not far enough extend,
(Since Rules were made but to promote their End)
Some Lucky LICENCE answers to the full
Th'Intent propos'd, *that Licence* is a *Rule.*
150 Thus *Pegasus,* a nearer way to take,
May boldly deviate from the common Track.
Great Wits sometimes may *gloriously offend,*
And *rise* to *Faults* true Criticks *dare not mend;*
From *vulgar Bounds* with *brave Disorder* part,
155 And *snatch* a *Grace* beyond the Reach of Art,
Which, without passing thro' the *Judgment,* gains
The *Heart,* and all its End *at once* attains.
In *Prospects,* thus, some *Objects* please our Eyes,
Which *out of* Nature's *common Order* rise,
160 The shapeless *Rock,* or hanging *Precipice.*
But tho' the *Ancients* thus their *Rules* invade,
(As *Kings* dispense with *Laws* Themselves have made)
Moderns, beware! Or if you must offend
Against the *Precept,* ne'er transgress its *End,*
165 Let it be *seldom,* and *compell'd by Need,*
And have, at least, *Their Precedent* to plead.
The Critick else proceeds without Remorse,
Seizes your Fame, and puts his Laws in force.
    I know there are, to whose presumptuous Thoughts
170 Those *Freer Beauties,* ev'n in *Them,* seem Faults:
Some Figures *monstrous* and *mis-shap'd* appear,

Consider'd *singly,* or beheld too *near,*
Which, but *proportion'd* to their *Light,* or *Place,*
Due Distance *reconciles* to Form and Grace.
175 A prudent Chief not always must display
His Pow'rs in *equal Ranks,* and *fair Array,*
But with th' *Occasion* and the *Place* comply,
Conceal his Force, nay seem sometimes to *Fly.*
Those oft are *Stratagems* which *Errors* seem,
180 Nor is it *Homer Nods,* but *We* that *Dream.*
　　　Still green with Bays each *ancient* Altar stands,
Above the reach of *Sacrilegious* Hands,
Secure from *Flames,* from *Envy's* fiercer Rage,
Destructive *War,* and all-involving *Age.*
185 See, from *each Clime* the Learn'd their Incense bring;
Hear, in *all Tongues* consenting *Pæans* ring!
In Praise so just, let ev'ry Voice be join'd,
And fill the *Gen'ral Chorus* of *Mankind*!
Hail *Bards Triumphant*! born in *happier Days;*
190 *Immortal* Heirs of *Universal* Praise!
Whose Honours with Increase of Ages *grow,*
As Streams roll down, *enlarging* as they flow!
Nations *unborn* your mighty Names shall sound,
And Worlds applaud that must not yet be *found*!
195 Oh may some Spark of *your* Cœlestial Fire
The last, the meanest of your Sons inspire,
(That on weak Wings, from far, pursues your Flights;
Glows while he *reads,* but *trembles* as he *writes*)
To teach vain Wits a Science *little known,*
200 T' *admire* Superior Sense, and *doubt* their own!

. . . .

Jonathan Swift

ON POETRY

A Rapsody

ALL Human Race wou'd fain be *Wits,*
And Millions miss, for one that hits.
Young's universal Passion, *Pride,*
Was never known to spread so wide.
5 Say *Britain,* cou'd you ever boast,——
Three *Poets* in an Age at most?
Our chilling Climate hardly bears
A *Sprig* of Bays in Fifty Years:
While ev'ry Fool his Claim alledges,
10 As if it grew in common Hedges.
What Reason can there be assign'd
For this Perverseness in the Mind?
Brutes find out where their Talents lie:
A *Bear* will not attempt to fly:
15 A founder'd *Horse* will oft debate,
Before he tries a five-barr'd Gate:
A *Dog* by Instinct turns aside,
Who sees the Ditch too deep and wide.
But *Man* we find the only Creature,
20 Who, led by *Folly,* fights with *Nature;*
Who, when *she* loudly cries, *Forbear,*
With Obstinacy fixes there;
And, where his *Genius* least inclines,
Absurdly bends his whole Designs.

25   Not *Empire* to the Rising-Sun,
By Valour, Conduct, Fortune won;
Nor highest *Wisdom* in Debates
For framing Laws to govern States;
Nor Skill in Sciences profound,
30 So large to grasp the Circle round;
Such heavenly Influence require,
As how to strike the *Muses Lyre.*

Not Beggar's Brat, on Bulk begot;
Nor Bastard of a Pedlar *Scot;*
35 Nor Boy brought up to cleaning Shoes,
The Spawn of *Bridewell,* or the Stews;
Nor Infants dropt, the spurious Pledges
Of *Gipsies* littering under Hedges,
Are so disqualified by Fate
40 To rise in *Church,* or *Law,* or *State,*
As he, whom *Phebus* in his Ire
Hath *blasted* with poetick Fire.

What hope of Custom in the *Fair,*
While not a Soul demands your Ware?
45 Where you have nothing to produce
For private Life, or publick Use?
Court, City, Country want you not;
You cannot bribe, betray, or plot.
For Poets, Law makes no Provision:
50 The Wealthy have you in Derision.
Of State-Affairs you cannot smatter,
Are awkward when you try to flatter.
Your Portion, taking *Britain* round,
*Was just one annual Hundred Pound.
55 Now not so much as in Remainder
Since *Cibber* brought in an Attainder;
For ever fixt by Right Divine,
(A Monarch's Right) on *Grubstreet* Line.
Poor starv'ling Bard, how small thy Gains!
60 How unproportion'd to thy Pains!

And here a *Simile* comes Pat in:
Tho' *Chickens* take a Month to fatten,
The Guests in less than half an Hour
Will more than half a Score devour.
65 So, after toiling twenty Days,
To earn a Stock of Pence and Praise,

---

* Paid to the Poet Laureat, which Place was given to one *Cibber,* a Player.

Thy Labours, grown the Critick's Prey,
Are swallow'd o'er a Dish of Tea;
Gone, to be never heard of more,
70 Gone, where the *Chickens* went before.

How shall a new Attempter learn
Of diff'rent Spirits to discern,
And how distinguish, which is which,
The Poet's Vein, or scribling Itch?
75 Then hear an old experienc'd Sinner
Instructing thus a young Beginner.

Consult yourself, and if you find
A powerful Impulse urge your Mind,
Impartial judge within your Breast
80 What Subject you can manage best;
Whether your Genius most inclines
To Satire, Praise, or hum'rous Lines;
To Elegies in mournful Tone,
Or Prologue sent from Hand unknown.

85 Then rising with *Aurora*'s Light,
The Muse invok'd, sit down to write;
Blot out, correct, insert, refine,
Enlarge, diminish, interline;
Be mindful, when Invention fails,
90 To scratch your Head, and bite your Nails.

Your Poem finish'd, next your Care
Is needful, to transcribe it fair.
In modern Wit all printed Trash, is
Set off with num'rous *Breaks*——and *Dashes*——

95 To Statesmen wou'd you give a Wipe,
You print it in *Italick Type*.
When Letters are in vulgar Shapes,
'Tis ten to one the Wit escapes;
But when in *Capitals* exprest,
100 The dullest Reader smoaks the Jest:
Or else perhaps he may invent

A better than the Poet meant,
As learned Commentators view
In *Homer* more than *Homer* knew.

105 Your Poem in its modish Dress,
Correctly fitted for the Press,
Convey by Penny-Post to *Lintot*,
But let no Friend alive look into't.
If *Lintot* thinks 'twill quit the Cost,

110 You need not fear your Labour lost:
And, how agreeably surpriz'd
Are you to see it advertiz'd!
The Hawker shews you one in Print,
As fresh as Farthings from the Mint:

115 The Product of your Toil and Sweating;
A Bastard of your own begetting.

Be sure at *Will's* the following Day,
Lie Snug, and hear what Criticks say.
And if you find the general Vogue

120 Pronounces you a stupid Rogue;
Damns all your Thoughts as low and little,
Sit still, and swallow down your Spittle.
Be silent as a Politician,
For talking may beget Suspicion:

125 Or praise the Judgment of the Town,
And help yourself to run it down.
Give up your fond paternal Pride,
Nor argue on the weaker Side;
For Poems read without a Name

130 We justly praise, or justly blame:
And Criticks have no partial Views,
Except they know whom they abuse.
And since you ne'er provok'd their Spight,
Depend upon't their Judgment's right:

135 But if you blab, you are undone;
Consider what a Risk you run.
You lose your Credit all at once;

The Town will mark you for a Dunce:
The vilest Doggrel *Grubstreet* sends,
140 Will pass for yours with Foes and Friends.
And you must bear the whole Disgrace,
'Till some fresh Blockhead takes your Place.

Your Secret kept, your Poem sunk,
And sent in Quires to line a Trunk;
145 If still you be dispos'd to rhime,
Go try your Hand a second Time.
Again you fail, yet Safe's the Word,
Take Courage, and attempt a Third.
But first with Care imploy your Thoughts,
150 Where Criticks mark'd your former Faults.
The trivial Turns, the borrow'd Wit,
The *Similes* that nothing fit;
The *Cant* which ev'ry Fool repeats,
Town-Jests, and Coffee-house Conceits;
155 Descriptions tedious, flat and dry,
And introduc'd the Lord knows why;
Or where we find your Fury set
Against the harmless Alphabet;
On A's and B's your Malice vent,
160 While Readers wonder whom you meant.
A publick, or a private *Robber;*
A *Statesman,* or a South-Sea *Jobber.*
A *Prelate* who no God believes;
A —¹, or Den of Thieves.
165 A Pick-purse at the Bar, or Bench;
A Duchess, or a Suburb-Wench.
Or oft when Epithets you link,
In gaping Lines to fill a Chink;
Like stepping Stones to save a Stride,
170 In Streets where Kennels are too wide:
Or like a Heel-piece to support

1 [Supply 'Parliament'.]

11

A Cripple with one Foot too short:
Or like a Bridge that joins a Marish
To Moorlands of a diff'rent Parish.
175 So have I seen ill-coupled Hounds,
Drag diff'rent Ways in miry Grounds.
So Geographers in *Afric*-Maps
With Savage-Pictures fill their Gaps;
And o'er unhabitable Downs
180 Place Elephants for want of Towns.

But tho' you miss your third Essay,
You need not throw your Pen away.
Lay now aside all Thoughts of Fame,
To spring more profitable Game.
185 From Party-Merit seek Support;
The vilest Verse thrives best at Court.
A Pamphlet in Sir *Rob*'s Defence
Will never fail to bring in Pence;
Nor be concern'd about the Sale,
190 He pays his Workmen on the Nail.

A Prince the Moment he is crown'd,
Inherits ev'ry Virtue round,
As Emblems of the sov'reign Pow'r,
Like other Bawbles of the Tow'r.
195 Is gen'rous, valiant, just and wise,
And so continues 'till he dies.
His humble *Senate* this professes,
In all their *Speeches, Votes, Addresses.*
But once you fix him in a Tomb,
200 His Virtues fade, his Vices bloom;
And each Perfection wrong imputed
Is Folly, at his Death confuted.
The Loads of Poems in his Praise,
Ascending make one Funeral-Blaze.
205 As soon as you can hear his Knell,
This God on Earth turns *Devil* in Hell.
And lo, his Ministers of State,

Transform'd to Imps, his Levee wait.
Where, in this Scene of endless Woe,
210 They ply their former Arts below.
And as they sail in *Charon's* Boat,
Contrive to bribe the Judge's Vote.
To *Cerberus* they give a Sop,
His triple-barking Mouth to Stop:
215 Or in the Iv'ry Gate of Dreams,
Project * * * and * * * * * * * [2]:
Or hire their Party-Pamphleteers,
To set *Elysium* by the Ears.

Then *Poet,* if you mean to thrive,
220 Employ your Muse on Kings alive;
With Prudence gath'ring up a Cluster
Of all the Virtues you can muster:
Which form'd into a Garland sweet,
Lay humbly at your Monarch's Feet;
225 Who, as the Odours reach his Throne,
Will smile, and think 'em all his own:
For *Law* and *Gospel* both determine
All Virtues lodge in royal Ermine.
(I mean the Oracles of Both,
230 Who shall depose it upon Oath.)
Your Garland in the following Reign,
Change but their Names will do again.

But if you think this Trade too base,
(Which seldom is the Dunce's Case)
235 Put on the Critick's Brow, and sit
At *Wills* the puny Judge of Wit.
A Nod, a Shrug, a scornful Smile,
With Caution us'd, may serve a-while.
Proceed no further in your Part,
240 Before you learn the Terms of Art:
(For you may easy be too far gone,

2 [The asterisks stand for 'Excise and South-Sea Schemes'.]

13

In all our modern Criticks Jargon.)
Then talk with more authentick Face,
Of *Unities, in Time and Place.*

245 Get Scraps of *Horace* from your Friends,
And have them at your Fingers Ends.
Learn *Aristotle*'s Rules by Rote,
And at all Hazards boldly quote:
Judicious *Rymer* oft review:

250 Wise *Dennis,* and profound *Bossu.*
Read all the *Prefaces* of *Dryden,*
For these our Criticks much confide in,
(Tho' meerly writ at first for filling
To raise the Volume's Price, a Shilling.)

255   A forward Critick often dupes us
With sham Quotations* *Peri Hupsous:*
And if we have not read *Longinus,*
Will magisterially out-shine us.
Then, lest with *Greek* he over-run ye,

260 Procure the Book for Love or Money,
Translated from *Boileau*'s Translation,**
And quote *Quotation* on *Quotation.*

     At *Wills* you hear a Poem read,
Where *Battus* from the Table-head,

265 Reclining on his Elbow-chair,
Gives Judgment with decisive Air.
To whom the Tribe of circling Wits,
As to an Oracle submits.
He gives Directions to the Town,

270 To cry it up, or run it down.
(Like *Courtiers,* when they send a Note,
Instructing *Members* how to Vote.)
He sets the Stamp of Bad and Good,
Tho' not a Word be understood.

275 Your Lesson learnt, you'll be secure

---

* A famous Treatise of Longinus. ** By Mr. *Welsted.*

To get the Name of *Conoisseur.*
And when your Merits once are known,
Procure Disciples of your own.

    Our Poets (you can never want 'em,
280 Spread thro' *Augusta Trinobantum*)
Computing by their Pecks of Coals,
Amount to just Nine thousand Souls.
These o'er their proper Districts govern,
Of Wit and Humour, Judges sov'reign.
285 In ev'ry Street a City-bard
Rules, like an Alderman his Ward.
His indisputed Rights extend
Thro' all the Lane, from End to End.
The Neighbours round admire his *Shrewdness,*
290 For songs of *Loyalty* and *Lewdness.*
Out-done by none in Rhyming well,
Altho' he never learnt to spell.

    Two bordering Wits contend for Glory;
And one is *Whig,* and one is *Tory.*
295 And this, for Epicks claims the Bays,
And that, for Elegiack Lays.
Some famed for Numbers soft and smooth,
By Lovers spoke in *Punch's* Booth.
And some as justly Fame extols
300 For lofty Lines in *Smithfield* Drols.
Bavius in *Wapping* gains Renown,
And *Mævius* reigns o'er *Kentish-Town:*
Tigellius plac'd in *Phœbus'* Car,
From *Ludgate* shines to *Temple-bar.*
305 Harmonius *Cibber* entertains
The Court with annual Birth-day Strains;
Whence *Gay* was banish'd in Disgrace,
Where *Pope* will never show his Face;
Where *Y[oung]* must torture his Invention,
310 To flatter *Knaves,* or lose his *Pension.*

But these are not a thousandth Part
Of Jobbers in the Poets Art,
Attending each his proper Station,
And all in due Subordination;
315 Thro' ev'ry Alley to be found,
In Garrets high, or under Ground:
And when they join their *Pericranies,*
Out skips a *Book of Miscellanies.*
Hobbes clearly proves that ev'ry Creature
320 Lives in a State of War by Nature.
The Greater for the Smallest watch,
But meddle seldom with their Match.
A Whale of moderate Size will draw
A Shole of Herrings down his Maw.
325 A Fox with Geese his Belly crams;
A Wolf destroys a thousand Lambs.
But search among the rhiming Race,
The Brave are worried by the Base.
If, on *Parnassus'* Top you sit,
330 You rarely bite, are always bit:
Each Poet of inferior Size
On you shall rail and criticize;
And strive to tear you Limb from Limb,
While others do as much for him.
335 The Vermin only teaze and pinch
Their Foes superior by an Inch.
So, Nat'ralists observe, a Flea
Hath smaller Fleas that on him prey,
And these have smaller Fleas to bite 'em,
340 And so proceed *ad infinitum:*
Thus ev'ry Poet in his Kind,
Is bit by him that comes behind;
Who, tho' too little to be seen,
Can teaze, and gall, and give the Spleen;
345 Call Dunces, Fools, and Sons of Whores,
Lay *Grubstreet* at each others Doors:
Extol the *Greek* and *Roman* Masters,

And curse our modern Poetasters.
Complain, as many an ancient Bard did,
350 How Genius is no more rewarded;
How wrong a Taste prevails among us;
How much our Ancestors out-sung us;
Can personate an awkward Scorn
For those who are not Poets born:
355 And all their Brother Dunces lash,
Who crowd the Press with hourly Trash.

O, *Grubstreet!* how do I bemoan thee,
Whose graceless Children scorn to own thee!
Their filial Piety forgot,
360 Deny their Country like a SCOT:
Tho' by their Idiom and Grimace
They soon betray their native Place:
Yet *thou* hast greater Cause to be
Asham'd of them, than they of thee.
365 Degenerate from their ancient Brood,
Since first the Court allow'd them Food.

Remains a Difficulty still,
To purchase Fame by writing ill:
From *Flecknoe* down to *Howard's* Time,
370 How few have reach'd the *low Sublime?*
For when our high-born *Howard* dy'd,
Blackmore alone his Place supply'd:
And least a Chasm should intervene,
When Death had finish'd *Blackmore's* Reign,
375 The *leaden Crown* devolv'd to thee,
Great Poet of the *Hollow-Tree.*
But, oh, how unsecure thy Throne!
A thousand Bards thy Right disown:
They plot to turn in factious Zeal,
380 *Duncenia* to a Common-weal;
And with rebellious Arms pretend
An equal Priv'lege to *descend.*

In Bulk there are not more Degrees,
From *Elephants* to *Mites* in Cheese,
385 Than what a curious Eye may trace
In Creatures of the rhiming Race.
From bad to worse, and worse they fall,
But, who can reach the Worst of all?
For, tho' in Nature Depth and Height
390 Are equally held infinite,
In Poetry the Height we know;
'Tis only infinite below.
For Instance: When you rashly *think,
No Rhymer can like *Welsted* sink.
395 His Merits ballanc'd you shall find,
That *Feilding* leaves him far behind.
Concannen, more aspiring Bard,
Climbs downwards, deeper by a Yard:
Smart JEMMY MOOR with Vigor drops,
400 The Rest pursue as thick as Hops:
With Heads to Points the Gulph they enter,
Linkt perpendicular to the Centre:
And as their Heels elated rise,
Their Heads attempt the nether Skies.

405   O, what Indignity and Shame
To prostitute the Muse's Name,
By flatt'ring —3 whom Heaven design'd
The Plagues and Scourges of Mankind.
Bred up in Ignorance and Sloth,
410 And ev'ry Vice that nurses both.

  Fair *Britain* in thy Monarch blest,
Whose Virtues bear the strictest Test;
Whom never *Faction* cou'd bespatter,
Nor *Minister,* nor *Poet* flatter.
415 What Justice in rewarding Merit?

* *Vide* The Treatise on the *Profound*, and Mr. *Pope's Dunciad*.
3 [Supply 'Kings'.]

18

What Magnanimity of Spirit?
What Lineaments divine we trace
Thro' all the Features of his Face;
Tho' Peace with Olive bind his Hands,
420 Confest the conqu'ring Hero stands.
Hydaspes, Indus, and the *Ganges,*
Dread from his Hand impending Changes.
From him the *Tartar,* and *Chinese,*
Short by the Knees intreat for Peace.
425 The *Consort* of his Throne and Bed,
A perfect Goddess born and bred.
Appointed sov'reign Judge to sit
On Learning, Eloquence and Wit.
Our eldest Hope, divine *Iülus,*
430 (Late, very late, O, may he rule us.)
What early Manhood has he shown,
Before his downy Beard was grown!
Then think, what Wonders will be done
By going on as he begun;
435 An Heir for *Britain* to secure
As long as Sun and Moon endure.

The Remnant of the royal Blood,
Comes pouring on me like a Flood.
Bright Goddesses, in Number five;
440 Duke *William,* sweetest Prince alive.

Now sing the *Minister* of *State,*
Who shines alone, without a Mate.
Observe with what majestick Port
This *Atlas* stands to prop the Court:
445 Intent the Publick Debts to pay,
Like prudent **Fabius* by *Delay.*
Thou great Vicegerent of the King,
Thy Praises ev'ry Muse shall sing.
In all Affairs thou sole Director,

---

* *Unus Homo nobis* Cunctando *restituit rem.*

450 Of Wit and Learning chief Protector;
　　Tho' small the Time thou hast to spare,
　　The Church is thy peculiar Care.
　　Of pious Prelates what a Stock
　　You chuse to rule the Sable-flock.
455 You raise the Honour of the Peerage,
　　Proud to attend you at the Steerage.
　　You dignify the noble Race,
　　Content yourself with humbler Place.
　　Now Learning, Valour, Virtue, Sense,
460 To Titles give the sole Pretence.
　　St. George beheld thee with Delight,
　　Vouchsafe to be an azure Knight,
　　When on thy Breast and Sides *Herculean,*
　　He fixt the *Star* and *String Cerulean.*

465 　　Say, Poet, in what other Nation,
　　Shone ever such a Constellation.
　　Attend ye *Popes,* and *Youngs,* and *Gays,*
　　And tune your Harps, and strow your Bays.
　　Your Panegyricks here provide,
470 You cannot err on Flatt'ry's Side.
　　Above the Stars exalt your Stile,
　　You still are low ten thousand Mile.
　　On *Lewis* all his Bards bestow'd,
　　Of Incense many a thousand Load;
475 But *Europe* mortify'd his Pride,
　　And swore the fawning Rascals ly'd:
　　Yet what the World refus'd to *Lewis,*
　　Apply'd to ⸺4 exactly true is:
　　Exactly true! Invidious Poet!
480 'Tis fifty thousand Times below it.

　　　　Translate me now some Lines, if you can,
　　From *Virgil, Martial, Ovid, Lucan;*
　　They could all Pow'r in Heaven divide,

4 [Supply 'George'.]

20

And do no Wrong to either Side:
485 They'll teach you how to split a Hair,
*Give --------[5] and *Jove* an equal Share.
Yet, why should we be lac'd so straight;
I'll give my * * * * *[6] Butter-weight.
And Reason good; for many a Year
490 -----[7] never intermeddl'd here:
Nor, tho' his Priests be duly paid,
Did ever we *desire* his Aid:
We now can better do without him,
Since *Woolston* gave us Arms to rout him.
* * * * * *Cætera desiderantur* * * * * *

---

* *Divisum Imperium cum* Jove Cæsar *habet.*

5 [Supply 'George'.]
6 [The asterisks stand for 'Monarch'.]
7 [Supply 'God' (or 'Jove').]

Alexander Pope

SPRING

[The First Pastoral]

To Sir *William Trumbull*

FIRST in these Fields I try the Sylvan Strains,
Nor blush to sport on *Windsor*'s blissful Plains:
Fair *Thames* flow gently from thy sacred Spring,
While on thy Banks *Sicilian* Muses sing;
5 Let Vernal Airs thro' trembling Osiers play,
And *Albion*'s Cliffs resound the Rural Lay.
You, that too Wise for Pride, too Good for Pow'r,
Enjoy the Glory to be Great no more,
And carrying with you all the World can boast,
10 To all the World Illustriously are lost!
O let my Muse her slender Reed inspire,
'Till in your Native Shades You tune the Lyre:
So when the Nightingale to Rest removes,
The Thrush may chant to the forsaken Groves,
15 But, charm'd to Silence, listens while She sings,
And all th'Aerial Audience clap their Wings.
Soon as the Flocks shook off the nightly Dews,
Two Swains, whom Love kept wakeful, and the Muse,
Pour'd o'er the whitening Vale their fleecy Care,
20 Fresh as the Morn, and as the Season fair:
The Dawn now blushing on the Mountain's Side,
Thus *Daphnis* spoke, and *Strephon* thus reply'd.

DAPHNIS.

Hear how the Birds, on ev'ry bloomy Spray,
With joyous Musick wake the dawning Day!
25 Why sit we mute, when early Linnets sing,
When warbling *Philomel* salutes the Spring?
Why sit we sad, when *Phosphor* shines so clear,
And lavish Nature paints the Purple Year?

STREPHON.

Sing then, and *Damon* shall attend the Strain,
30 While yon slow Oxen turn the furrow'd Plain.
Here the bright Crocus and blue Vi'let glow;
Here Western Winds on breathing Roses blow.
I'll stake yon' Lamb that near the Fountain plays,
And from the Brink his dancing Shade surveys.

DAPHNIS.

35 And I this Bowl, where wanton Ivy twines,
And swelling Clusters bend the curling Vines:
Four Figures rising from the Work appear,
The various Seasons of the rowling Year;
And what is That, which binds the Radiant Sky,
40 Where twelve fair Signs in beauteous Order lye?

DAMON.

Then sing by turns, by turns the Muses sing,
Now Hawthorns blossom, now the Daisies spring,
Now Leaves the Trees, and Flow'rs adorn the Ground;
Begin, the Vales shall ev'ry Note rebound.

STREPHON.

45 Inspire me *Phœbus,* in my *Delia'*s Praise,
With *Waller'*s Strains, or *Granville'*s moving Lays!
A Milk-white Bull shall at your Altars stand,
That threats a Fight, and spurns the rising Sand.

DAPHNIS.

O Love! for *Sylvia* let me gain the Prize,
50 And make my Tongue victorious as her Eyes;

No Lambs or Sheep for Victims I'll impart,
Thy Victim, Love, shall be the Shepherd's Heart.

STREPHON.
Me gentle *Delia* beckons from the Plain,
Then hid in Shades, eludes her eager Swain;
55 But feigns a Laugh, to see me search around,
And by that Laugh the willing Fair is found.

DAPHNIS.
The sprightly *Sylvia* trips along the Green,
She runs, but hopes she does not run unseen,
While a kind Glance at her Pursuer flies,
60 How much at variance are her Feet and Eyes!

STREPHON.
O'er Golden Sands let rich *Pactolus* flow,
And Trees weep Amber on the Banks of *Po;*
Blest *Thames*'s Shores the brightest Beauties yield,
Feed here my Lambs, I'll seek no distant Field.

DAPHNIS.
65 Celestial *Venus* haunts *Idalia's* Groves,
Diana Cynthus, Ceres Hybla loves;
If *Windsor*-Shades delight the matchless Maid,
Cynthus and *Hybla* yield to *Windsor*-Shade.

STREPHON.
All Nature mourns, the Skies relent in Show'rs,
70 Hush'd are the Birds, and clos'd the drooping Flow'rs;
If *Delia* smile, the Flow'rs begin to spring,
The Skies to brighten, and the Birds to sing.

DAPHNIS.
All Nature laughs, the Groves are fresh and fair,
The Sun's mild Lustre warms the vital Air;
75 If *Sylvia* smiles, new Glories gild the Shore,
And vanquish'd Nature seems to charm no more.

STREPHON.

In Spring the Fields, in Autumn Hills I love,
At Morn the Plains, at Noon the shady Grove;
But *Delia* always; absent from her Sight,
80   Nor Plains at Morn, nor Groves at Noon delight.

DAPHNIS.

Sylvia's like Autumn ripe, yet mild as *May,*
More bright than Noon, yet fresh as early Day,
Ev'n Spring displeases, when she shines not here,
But blest with her, 'tis Spring throughout the Year.

STREPHON.

85   Say, *Daphnis,* say, in what glad Soil appears
A wondrous *Tree* that Sacred *Monarchs* bears?
Tell me but this, and I'll disclaim the Prize,
And give the Conquest to thy *Sylvia's* Eyes.

DAPHNIS.

Nay tell me first, in what more happy Fields
90   The *Thistle* springs, to which the *Lilly* yields?
And then a nobler Prize I will resign,
For *Sylvia,* charming *Sylvia* shall be thine.

DAMON.

Cease to contend, for *(Daphnis)* I decree
The Bowl to *Strephon,* and the Lamb to thee:
95   Blest Swains, whose Nymphs in ev'ry Grace excell;
Blest Nymphs, whose Swains those Graces sing so well!
Now rise, and haste to yonder Woodbine Bow'rs,
A soft Retreat from sudden vernal Show'rs;
The Turf with rural Dainties shall be Crown'd,
100   While opening Blooms diffuse their Sweets around.
For see! the gath'ring Flocks to Shelter tend,
And from the *Pleiads* fruitful Show'rs descend.

John Gay

SATURDAY OR THE FLIGHTS

[From *The Shepherd's* Week]

BOWZYBEUS.

SUBLIMER strains, O rustick Muse, prepare;
Forget a-while the barn and dairy's care;
Thy homely voice to loftier numbers raise,
The drunkard's flights require sonorous lays,
5   With *Bowzybeus'* songs exalt thy verse,
While rocks and woods the various notes rehearse.
   'Twas in the season when the reapers toil
Of the ripe harvest 'gan to rid the soil;
Wide through the field was seen a goodly rout,
10 Clean damsels bound the gather'd sheaves about,
The lads with sharpen'd hook and sweating brow
Cut down the labours of the winter plow.
To the near hedge young *Susan* steps aside,
She feign'd her coat or garter was unty'd,
15 What-e'er she did, she stoop'd adown unseen,
And merry reapers, what they list, will ween.
Soon she rose up, and cry'd with voice so shrill
That eccho answer'd from the distant hill;
The youths and damsels ran to *Susan's* aid,
20 Who thought some adder had the lass dismay'd.
   There fast asleep they *Bowzybeus* spy'd,
His hat and oaken staff lay close beside.
That *Bowzybeus* who could sweetly sing,
Or with the rozin'd bow torment the string;
25 That *Bowzybeus* who with finger's speed
Could call soft warblings from the breathing reed;
That *Bowzybeus* who with jocond tongue,
Ballads and roundelays and catches sung.
They loudly laugh to see the damsel's fright,
30 And in disport surround the drunken wight.
   Ah *Bowzybee,* why didst thou stay so long?

The mugs were large, the drink was wondrous strong!
Thou should'st have left the Fair before 'twas night,
But thou sat'st toping 'till the morning light.
35   *Cic'ly,* brisk maid, steps forth before the rout,
And kiss'd with smacking lip the snoring lout.
For custom says, *Whoe'er this venture proves,*
For such a kiss demands a pair of gloves.
By her example *Dorcas* bolder grows,
40   And plays a tickling straw within his nose.
He rubs his nostril, and in wonted joke
The sneering swains with stamm'ring speech bespoke.
To you, my lads, I'll sing my carrol's o'er,
As for the maids,—I've something else in store.
45   No sooner 'gan he raise his tuneful song,
But lads and lasses round about him throng.
Not ballad-singer plac'd above the croud
Sings with a note so shrilling sweet and loud,
Nor parish-clerk who calls the psalm so clear,
50   Like *Bowzybeus* sooths th' attentive ear.
       Of nature's laws his carrols first begun,
Why the grave owle can never face the sun.
For owles, as swains observe, detest the light,
And only sing and seek their prey by night.
55   How turnips hide their swelling heads below,
And how the closing colworts upwards grow;
How *Will-a-Wisp* mis-leads night-faring clowns,
O'er hills, and sinking bogs, and pathless downs.
Of stars he told that shoot with shining trail,
60   And of the glow-worm's light that gilds his tail.
He sung where wood-cocks in the summer feed,
And in what climates they renew their breed;
Some think to northern coasts their flight they tend,
Or to the moon in midnight hours ascend.
65   Where swallows in the winter's season keep,
And how the drowsie bat and dormouse sleep.
How nature does the puppy's eyelid close,
'Till the bright sun has nine times set and rose.

For huntsmen by their long experience find,
70 That puppys still nine rolling suns are blind.
      Now he goes on, and sings of Fairs and shows,
    For still new fairs before his eyes arose.
    How pedlars stalls with glitt'ring toys are laid,
    The various fairings of the country maid.
75 Long silken laces hang upon the twine,
    And rows of pins and amber bracelets shine;
    How the tight lass, knives, combs, and scissars spys,
    And looks on thimbles with desiring eyes.
    Of lott'ries next with tuneful note he told,
80 Where silver spoons are won and rings of gold.
    The lads and lasses trudge the street along,
    And all the fair is crouded in his song.
    The mountebank now treads the stage, and sells
    His pills, his balsams, and his ague-spells;
85 Now o'er and o'er the nimble tumbler springs,
    And on the rope the ventrous maiden swings;
    Jack Pudding in his parti-colour'd jacket
    Tosses the glove, and jokes at ev'ry packet.
    Of *Raree-shows* he sung, and *Punch's* feats,
90 Of pockets pick'd in crowds, and various cheats.
      Then sad he sung *the Children in the Wood.*
    Ah barb'rous uncle, stain'd with infant blood!
    How blackberrys they pluck'd in desarts wild,
    And fearless at the glittering fauchion smil'd;
95 Their little corps the robin-red-breasts found,
    And strow'd with pious bill the leaves around.
    Ah gentle birds! if this verse lasts so long,
    Your names shall live for ever in my song.
      For buxom *Joan* he sung the doubtful strife,
100 How the sly sailor made the maid a wife.
      To louder strains he rais'd his voice, to tell
    What woeful wars in *Chevy-chace* befell,
    When *Piercy drove the deer with hound and horn,*
    Wars to be wept by children yet unborn!
105 Ah *With'rington,* more years thy life had crown'd,

If thou hadst never heard the horn or hound!
Yet shall the Squire who fought on bloody stumps,
By future bards be wail'd in doleful dumps.
   All in the land of Essex next he chaunts,
110 How to sleek mares starch quakers turn gallants;
How the grave brother stood on bank so green.
Happy for him if mares had never been!
   Then he was seiz'd with a religious qualm,
And on a sudden, sung the hundredth psalm.
115   He sung of *Taffey Welch,* and *Sawney Scot,*
Lilly-bullero and the *Irish Trot.*
Why should I tell of *Bateman* or of *Shore,*
Or *Wantley's Dragon* slain by valiant *Moore,*
The bow'r of Rosamond, or *Robin Hood,*
120 And how the *grass now grows where* Troy town *stood*?
   His carrols ceas'd: the list'ning maids and swains
Seem still to hear some soft imperfect strains.
Sudden he rose; and as he reels along
Swears kisses sweet should well reward his song.
125 The damsels laughing fly: the giddy clown
Again upon a wheat-sheaf drops adown;
The pow'r that guards the drunk, his sleep attends,
'Till, ruddy, like his face, the sun descends.

Jonathan Swift

A DESCRIPTION OF A CITY SHOWER[1]

CAREFUL Observers may fortel the Hour
(By sure Prognosticks) when to dread a Show'r:
While Rain depends, the pensive Cat gives o'er
Her Frolicks, and pursues her Tail no more.
5 Returning Home at Night, you'll find the Sink

---

1 [Several early editions added to the title the words: *'In Imitation of*
VIRGIL's Georg.']

Strike your offended Sense with double Stink.
If you be wise, then go not far to Dine,
You'll spend in Coach-hire more than save in Wine.
A coming Show'r your shooting Corns presage,
10   Old Aches throb, your hollow Tooth will rage.
Sauntring in Coffee-house is *Dulman* seen;
He damns the Climate, and complains of Spleen.

MEAN while the South rising with dabbled Wings,
A Sable Cloud a-thwart the Welkin flings,
15   That swill'd more Liquor than it could contain,
And like a Drunkard gives it up again.
Brisk *Susan* whips her Linen from the Rope,
While the first drizzling Show'r is born aslope,
Such is that Sprinkling which some careless Quean
20   Flirts on you from her Mop, but not so clean.
You fly, invoke the Gods; then turning, stop
To rail; she singing, still whirls on her Mop.
Not yet, the Dust had shun'd th' unequal Strife,
But aided by the Wind, fought still for Life;
25   And wafted with its Foe by violent Gust,
'Twas doubtful which was Rain, and which was Dust.
Ah! where must needy Poet seek for Aid,
When Dust and Rain at once his Coat invade;
His only Coat, where Dust confus'd with Rain,
30   Roughen the Nap, and leave a mingled Stain.

NOW in contiguous Drops the Flood comes down,
Threat'ning with Deluge this *Devoted* Town.
To Shops in Crouds the dagged Females fly,
Pretend to cheapen Goods, but nothing buy.
35   The Templer spruce, while ev'ry Spout's a-broach,
Stays till 'tis fair, yet seems to call a Coach.
The tuck'd-up Sempstress walks with hasty Strides,
While Streams run down her oil'd Umbrella's Sides.
Here various Kinds by various Fortunes led,
40   Commence Acquaintance underneath a Shed.
Triumphant Tories, and desponding Whigs,

Forget their Fewds, and join to save their Wigs.
Box'd in a Chair the Beau impatient sits,
While Spouts run clatt'ring o'er the Roof by Fits;
45   And ever and anon with frightful Din
The Leather sounds, he trembles from within.
So when *Troy* Chair-men bore the Wooden Steed,
Pregnant with *Greeks,* impatient to be freed,
(Those Bully *Greeks,* who, as the Moderns do,
50   Instead of paying Chair-men, run them thro'.)
Laoco'n struck the Outside with his Spear,
And each imprison'd Hero quak'd for Fear.

NOW from all Parts the swelling Kennels flow,
And bear their Trophies with them as they go:
55   Filth of all Hues and Odours seem to tell
What Street they sail'd from, by their Sight and Smell.
They, as each Torrent drives, with rapid Force
From *Smithfield,* or St. *Pulchre*'s shape their Course,
And in huge Confluent join at *Snow-Hill* Ridge,
60   Fall from the *Conduit* prone to *Holborn-Bridge.*
Sweepings from Butchers Stalls, Dung, Guts, and Blood,
Drown'd Puppies, stinking Sprats, all drench'd in Mud,
Dead Cats and Turnip-Tops come tumbling down the Flood.

Jonathan Swift

STREPHON AND CHLOE

OF *Chloe* all the Town has rung;
By ev'ry size of Poets sung:
So beautiful a Nymph appears
But once in Twenty Thousand Years.
5   By Nature form'd with nicest Care,
And, faultless to a single Hair.
Her graceful Mein, her Shape, and Face,

Confest her of no mortal Race:
And then, so nice, and so genteel;
10 Such Cleanliness from Head to Heel:
No Humours gross, or frowzy Steams,
No noisom Whiffs, or sweaty Streams,
Before, behind, above, below,
Could from her taintless Body flow.
15 Would so discreetly Things dispose,
None ever saw her pluck a Rose.
Her dearest Comrades never caught her
Squat on her Hams, to make Maid's Water.
You'd swear, that so divine a Creature
20 Felt no Necessities of Nature.
In Summer had she walkt the Town,
Her Arm-pits would not stain her Gown:
At Country Dances, not a Nose
Could in the Dog-Days smell her Toes.
25 Her Milk-white Hands, both Palms and Backs,
Like Iv'ry dry, and soft as Wax.
Her Hands the softest ever felt,
Tho' cold would burn, tho' dry would melt.
   DEAR *Venus,* hide this wond'rous Maid,
30 Nor let her loose to spoil your Trade.
While she engrosseth ev'ry Swain,
You but o'er half the World can reign.
Think what a Case all Men are now in,
What ogling, sighing, toasting, vowing!
35 What powder'd Wigs! What Flames and Darts!
What Hampers full of bleeding Hearts!
What Sword-knots! What Poetic Strains!
What Billet-doux, and clouded Cains!
   BUT, *Strephon* sigh'd so loud and strong,
40 He blew a Settlement along:
And, bravely drove his Rivals down
With Coach and Six, and House in Town.
The bashful Nymph no more withstands,
Because her dear Papa commands.

45 The charming Couple now unites;
   Proceed we to the Marriage Rites.
        IMPRIMIS, at the Temple Porch
   Stood *Hymen* with a flaming Torch.
   The smiling *Cyprian* Goddess brings
50 Her infant Loves with purple Wings;
   And Pigeons billing, Sparrows treading,
   Fair Emblems of a fruitful Wedding.
   The Muses next in Order follow,
   Conducted by their Squire, *Apollo:*
55 Then *Mercury* with Silver Tongue,
   And *Hebe,* Goddess ever young.
   Behold the Bridegroom and his Bride,
   Walk Hand in Hand, and Side by Side;
   She by the tender Graces drest,
60 But, he by *Mars,* in Scarlet Vest.
   The Nymph was cover'd with her **Flammeum,*
   And *Phœbus* sung th' *Epithalamium.*
   And, last to make the Matter sure,
   Dame *Juno* brought a Priest demure.
65 ***Luna* was absent on Pretence
   Her Time was not till Nine Months hence.
        THE Rites perform'd, the Parson paid,
   In State return'd the grand Parade;
   With loud Huzza's from all the Boys,
70 That now the Pair must *crown their Joys.*
        BUT, still the hardest Part remains.
   Strephon had long perplex'd his Brains,
   How with so high a Nymph he might
   Demean himself the Wedding-Night:
75 For, as he view'd his Person round,
   Meer mortal Flesh was all he found:
   His Hand, his Neck, his Mouth, and Feet

* A Veil which the *Roman* Brides covered themselves with, when they were
   going to be married.
** *Diana,* Goddess of Midwives.

Were duly washt to keep 'em sweet;
(With other Parts that shall be nameless,
80   The Ladies else might think me shameless.)
The Weather and his Love were hot;
And should he struggle; I know what—
Why let it go, if I must tell it—
He'll sweat, and then the Nymph may smell it.
85   While she a Goddess dy'd in Grain
Was unsusceptible of Stain:
And, *Venus*-like, her fragrant Skin
Exhal'd *Ambrosia* from within:
Can such a Deity endure
90   A mortal human Touch impure?
How did the humbled Swain detest
His prickled Beard, and hairy Breast!
His Night-Cap border'd round with Lace
Could give no Softness to his Face.
95   YET, if the Goddess could be kind,
What endless Raptures must he find!
And Goddesses have now and then
Come down to visit mortal Men:
To visit and to court them too;
100   A certain Goddess, God knows who,
(As in a Book he heard it read)
Took Col'nel *Peleus* to her Bed.
But, what if he should lose his Life
By vent'ring *on* his heav'nly Wife?
105   For *Strephon* could remember well,
That, once he heard a School-boy tell,
How *Semele* of mortal Race,
By Thunder dy'd in *Jove*'s Embrace;
And what if daring *Strephon* dies
110   By Lightning shot from *Chloe*'s Eyes?
    WHILE these Reflections fill'd his Head,
The Bride was put in Form to Bed;
He follow'd, stript, and in he crept,
But, awfully his Distance kept.

115   Now, *Ponder well ye Parents dear;*
      Forbid your Daughters guzzling Beer;
      And make them ev'ry Afternoon
      Forbear their Tea, or drink it soon;
      That, e'er to Bed they venture up,
120   They may discharge it ev'ry Sup;
      If not; they must in evil Plight
      Be often forc'd to rise at Night,
      Keep them to wholsome Food confin'd,
      Nor let them taste what causes Wind;
125   *('Tis this the Sage of *Samos* means,
      Forbidding his Disciples Beans)
      O, think what Evils must ensue;
      Miss *Moll* the Jade will burn it blue:
      And when she once has got the Art,
130   She cannot help it for her Heart;
      But, out it flies, even when she meets
      Her Bridegroom in the Wedding-Sheets.
      ** *Carminative* and ***Diuretick,*
      Will damp all Passion Sympathetick;
135   And, Love such Nicety requires,
      One *Blast* will put out all his Fires.
      Since Husbands get behind the Scene,
      The Wife should study to be clean;
      Nor give the smallest Room to guess
140   The Time when Wants of Nature press;
        BUT, after Marriage, practise more
      Decorum than she did before;
      To keep her Spouse deluded still,
      And make him fancy what she will.
145   IN Bed we left the married Pair;
      'Tis Time to shew how Things went there.
      Strephon, who had been often told,

* A well known Precept of *Pythagoras,* not to eat Beans.
** Medicines to break Wind,
*** Medicines to provoke Urine.

That Fortune still assists the bold,
Resolv'd to make his first Attack:
150   But, *Chloe* drove him fiercely back.
How could a Nymph so chaste as *Chloe,*
With Constitution cold and snowy,
Permit a brutish Man to touch her?
Ev'n Lambs by Instinct fly the Butcher.
155   Resistance on the Wedding-Night
Is what our Maidens claim by Right:
And, *Chloe,* 'tis by all agreed,
Was Maid in Thought, and Word, and Deed,
Yet, some assign a diff'rent Reason;
160   That *Strephon* chose no proper Season.
     S A Y , fair ones, must I make a Pause?
Or freely tell the secret Cause.
     T W E L V E Cups of Tea, (with Grief I speak)
Had now constrain'd the Nymph to leak.
165   This Point must needs be settled first;
The Bride must either void or burst.
Then, see the dire Effect of Pease,
Think what can give the Colick Ease,
The Nymph opprest before, behind,
170   As Ships are toss't by Waves and Wind,
Steals out her Hand by Nature led,
And brings a Vessel into Bed:
Fair Utensil, as smooth and white
As *Chloe'*s Skin, almost as bright.
175   *STREPHON* who heard the fuming Rill
As from a mossy Cliff distill;
Cry'd out, ye Gods, what Sound is this?
Can *Chloe,* heav'nly *Chloe*— ?
But, when he smelt a noysom Steam
180   Which oft attends that luke-warm Stream;
(*Salerno** both together joins
As sov'reign Med'cines for the Loins)

---

* Vide Schol. *Salern. Rules of Health, written by the School of* Salernum.
Mingere cum bumbis res est saluberrima lumbis.

And, though contriv'd, we may suppose
To slip his Ears, yet struck his Nose:
185 He found her, while the Scent increas'd,
As *mortal* as himself at least.
But, soon with like Occasions prest,
He boldly sent his Hand in quest,
(Inspir'd with Courage from his Bride,)
190 To reach the Pot on t'other Side.
And as he fill'd the reeking Vase,
Let fly a Rouzer in her Face.

THE little *Cupids* hov'ring round,
(As Pictures prove) with Garlands crown'd,
195 Abasht at what they saw and heard,
Flew off, nor evermore appear'd.

ADIEU to ravishing Delights,
High Raptures, and romantick Flights;
To Goddesses so heav'nly sweet,
200 Expiring Shepherds at their Feet;
To silver Meads, and shady Bow'rs,
Drest up with *Amaranthine* Flow'rs.

How great a Change! how quickly made!
They learn to call a Spade, a Spade.
205 They soon from all Constraint are freed;
Can see each other *do their Need.*
On Box of Cedar sits the Wife,
And makes it warm for *Dearest Life.*
And, by the beastly way of Thinking,
210 Find great Society in Stinking.
Now *Strephon* daily entertains
His *Chloe* in the homeli'st Strains;
And, *Chloe* more experienc'd grown,
With Int'rest pays him back his own.
215 No Maid at Court is less asham'd,
Howe'er for selling Bargains fam'd,
Than she, to name her Parts behind,
Or when a-bed, to let out Wind.

FAIR *Decency,* celestial Maid,

220 Descend from Heav'n to Beauty's Aid;
Though Beauty may beget Desire,
'Tis thou must fan the Lover's Fire;
For, Beauty, like supreme Dominion,
Is best supported by Opinion;
225 If Decency brings no Supplies,
Opinion falls, and Beauty dies.

To see some radiant Nymph appear
In all her glitt'ring Birth-day Gear,
You think some Goddess from the Sky
230 Descended, ready cut and dry:
But, e'er you sell your self to Laughter,
Consider well what may come after;
For fine Ideas vanish fast,
While all the gross and filthy last.
235 O *Strephon,* e'er that fatal Day
When *Chloe* stole your Heart away,
Had you but through a Cranny spy'd
On House of Ease your future Bride,
In all the Postures of her Face,
240 Which Nature gives in such a Case;
Distortions, Groanings, Strainings, Heavings;
'Twere better you had lickt her Leavings,
Than from Experience find too late
Your Goddess grown a filthy Mate.
245 Your Fancy then had always dwelt
On what you saw, and what you smelt;
Would still the same Ideas give ye,
As when you spy'd her on the Privy.
And, spight of *Chloe'*s Charms divine,
250 Your Heart had been as whole as mine.
AUTHORITIES both old and recent
Direct that Women must be decent;
And, from the Spouse each Blemish hide
More than from all the World beside.
255 UNJUSTLY all our Nymphs complain,
Their Empire holds so short a Reign;

Is after Marriage lost so soon,
It hardly holds the Honey-moon:
For, if they keep not what they caught,
260 It is entirely their own Fault.
They take Possession of the Crown,
And then throw all their Weapons down;
Though by the Politicians Scheme
Whoe'er arrives at Pow'r supreme,
265 Those Arts by which at first they gain it,
They still must practise to maintain it.
    WHAT various Ways our Females take,
To pass for Wits before a Rake!
And in the fruitless Search pursue
270 All other Methods but the true.
    SOME try to learn polite Behaviour,
By reading Books against their Saviour;
Some call it witty to reflect
On ev'ry natural Defect;
275 Some shew they never want explaining,
To comprehend a double Meaning.
But, sure a Tell-tale out of School
Is of all Wits the greatest Fool;
Whose rank Imagination fills,
280 Her Heart, and from her Lips distills;
You'd think she utter'd from behind,
Or at her Mouth was breaking Wind.
    WHY is a handsome Wife ador'd
By ev'ry Coxcomb, but her Lord?
285 From yonder Puppet-Man inquire,
Who wisely hides his Wood and Wire;
Shews *Sheba*'s Queen completely drest,
And *Solomon* in Royal Vest;
But, view them litter'd on the Floor,
290 Or strung on Pegs behind the Door;
Punch is exactly of a Piece
With *Lorraine*'s Duke, and Prince of *Greece*.
    A PRUDENT Builder should forecast

How long the Stuff is like to last;
295 And carefully observe the Ground,
To build on some Foundation sound;
What House, when its Materials crumble,
Must not inevitably tumble?
What Edifice can long endure,
300 Rais'd on a Basis unsecure?
Rash Mortals, e'er you take a Wife,
Contrive your Pile to last for Life;
Since Beauty scarce endures a Day,
And Youth so swiftly glides away;
305 Why will you make yourself a Bubble
To build on Sand with Hay and Stubble?
    ON Sense and Wit your Passion found,
By Decency cemented round;
Let Prudence with Good Nature strive,
310 To keep Esteem and Love alive.
Then come old Age whene'er it will,
Your Friendship shall continue still:
And thus a mutual gentle Fire,
Shall never but with Life expire.

James Thomson

WINTER

A Poem

SEE! WINTER comes, to rule the varied Year,
Sullen, and sad; with all his rising Train,
Vapours, and *Clouds,* and *Storms:* Be these my Theme,
These, that exalt the Soul to solemn Thought,
5 And heavenly musing. Welcome kindred Glooms!
Wish'd, wint'ry, Horrors, hail!—With frequent Foot,
Pleas'd, have I, in my cheerful Morn of Life,
When, nurs'd by careless *Solitude,* I liv'd,

And sung of Nature with unceasing Joy,
10 Pleas'd, have I wander'd thro' your rough Domains;
    Trod the pure, virgin, Snows, myself as pure:
    Heard the Winds roar, and the big Torrent burst:
    Or seen the deep, fermenting, Tempest brew'd,
    In the red, evening, Sky.—Thus pass'd the Time,
15 Till, thro' the opening Chambers of the South,
    Look'd out the joyous *Spring,* look'd out, and smil'd.

    THEE too, Inspirer of the toiling Swain!
    Fair AUTUMN, yellow rob'd! I'll sing of thee,
    Of thy last, temper'd, Days, and sunny Calms;
20 When all the golden *Hours* are on the Wing,
    Attending thy Retreat, and round thy Wain,
    Slow-rolling, onward to the Southern Sky.

    BEHOLD! the well-pois'd *Hornet,* hovering, hangs,
    With quivering Pinions, in the genial Blaze;
25 Flys off, in airy Circles: then returns,
    And hums, and dances to the beating Ray.
    Nor shall the Man, that, musing, walks alone,
    And, heedless, strays within his radiant Lists,
    Go unchastis'd away.—Sometimes, a Fleece
30 Of Clouds, wide-scattering, with a lucid Veil,
    Soft, shadow o'er th' unruffled Face of Heaven;
    And, thro' their dewy Sluices, shed the Sun,
    With temper'd Influence down. Then is the Time,
    For those, whom *Wisdom,* and whom *Nature* charm,
35 To steal themselves from the degenerate Croud,
    And soar above this *little* Scene of Things:
    To tread low-thoughted *Vice* beneath their Feet:
    To lay their Passions in a gentle Calm,
    And woo lone *Quiet,* in her silent *Walks.*

40 NOW, solitary, and in pensive Guise,
    Oft, let me wander o'er the russet Mead,
    Or thro' the pining Grove; where scarce is heard
    One dying Strain, to chear the *Woodman's* Toil:

Sad *Philomel,* perchance, pours forth her Plaint,
45 Far, thro' the withering Copse. Mean while, the Leaves,
That, late, the Forest clad with lively Green,
Nipt by the drizzly Night, and Sallow-hu'd,
Fall, wavering, thro' the Air; or shower amain,
Urg'd by the Breeze, that sobs amid the Boughs.
50 Then listening *Hares* forsake the rusling Woods,
And, starting at the frequent Noise, escape
To the rough Stubble, and the rushy Fen.
Then *Woodcocks,* o'er the fluctuating Main,
That glimmers to the Glimpses of the Moon,
55 Stretch their long Voyage to the woodland Glade
Where, wheeling with uncertain Flight, they mock
The nimble *Fowler's* Aim.—Now *Nature* droops;
Languish the living Herbs, with pale Decay:
And all the *various Family* of Flowers
60 Their sunny Robes resign. The falling Fruits,
Thro' the still Night, forsake the Parent-Bough,
That, in the first, grey, Glances of the Dawn,
Looks wild, and wonders at the wintry Waste.

THE *Year,* yet pleasing, but declining fast,
65 Soft, o'er the secret Soul, in gentle Gales,
A Philosophic Melancholly breathes,
And bears the swelling Thought aloft to Heaven.
Then forming *Fancy* rouses to conceive,
What never mingled with the Vulgar's Dream:
70 Then wake the tender *Pang,* the pitying *Tear,*
The *Sigh* for suffering Worth, the *Wish* prefer'd
For Humankind, the *Joy* to see them bless'd,
And all the *Social Off-spring* of the Heart!

OH! bear me then to high, embowering, Shades;
75 To twilight Groves, and visionary Vales;
To weeping Grottos, and to hoary Caves;
Where Angel-Forms are seen, and Voices heard,

Sigh'd in low Whispers, that abstract the Soul,
From outward Sense, far into Worlds remote.

80   NOW, when the Western Sun withdraws the Day,
And humid *Evening,* gliding o'er the Sky,
In her chill Progress, checks the straggling Beams,
And robs them of their gather'd, vapoury, Prey,
Where Marshes stagnate, and where Rivers wind,
85   Cluster the rolling *Fogs,* and swim along
The dusky-mantled Lawn: then slow descend,
Once more to mingle with their *Watry Friends.*

THE vivid Stars shine out, in radiant Files;
And boundless *Ether* glows, till the fair Moon
90   Shows her broad Visage, in the crimson'd East;
Now, stooping, seems to kiss the passing Cloud:
Now, o'er the pure *Cerulean,* rides sublime.
Wide the pale Deluge floats, with silver Waves,
O'er the sky'd Mountain, to the low-laid Vale;
95   From the white Rocks, with dim Reflexion, gleams,
And faintly glitters thro' the waving Shades.

ALL Night, abundant Dews, unnoted, fall,
And, at Return of Morning, silver o'er
The Face of Mother-Earth; from every Branch
100 Depending, tremble the translucent Gems,
And, quivering, seem to fall away, yet cling,
And sparkle in the Sun, whose rising Eye,
With Fogs bedim'd, portends a beauteous Day.

NOW, giddy Youth, whom headlong Passions fire,
105 Rouse the wild Game, and stain the guiltless Grove,
With Violence, and Death; yet call it Sport,
To scatter Ruin thro' the Realms of *Love,*
And *Peace,* that thinks no ill: But These, the *Muse,*
Whose Charity, unlimited, extends
110 As wide as *Nature* works, disdains to sing,
Returning to her nobler Theme in view—

FOR see! where *Winter* comes, himself, confest,
Striding the gloomy Blast. First Rains obscure
Drive thro' the mingling Skies, with Tempest foul;
115   Beat on the Mountain's Brow, and shake the Woods,
That, sounding, wave below. The dreary Plain
Lies overwhelm'd, and lost. The bellying Clouds
Combine, and deepening into Night, shut up
The Day's fair Face. The Wanderers of Heaven,
120   Each to his Home, retire; save those that love
To take their Pastime in the troubled Air,
And, skimming, flutter round the dimply Flood.
The Cattle, from th' untasted Fields, return,
And ask, with Meaning low, their wonted Stalls;
125   Or ruminate in the contiguous Shade:
Thither, the houshold, feathery, People croud,
The crested Cock, with all his female Train,
Pensive, and wet. Mean while, the Cottage-Swain
Hangs o'er th' enlivening Blaze, and, taleful, there,
130   Recounts his simple Frolic: Much he talks,
And much he laughs, nor recks the Storm that blows
Without, and rattles on his humble Roof.

AT last, the muddy Deluge pours along,
Resistless, roaring; dreadful down it comes
135   From the chapt Mountain, and the mossy Wild,
Tumbling thro' Rocks abrupt, and sounding far:
Then o'er the sanded Valley, floating, spreads,
Calm, sluggish, silent; till again constrain'd,
Betwixt two meeting Hills, it bursts a Way,
140   Where Rocks, and Woods o'erhang the turbid Stream.
There gathering triple Force, rapid, and deep,
It boils, and wheels, and foams, and thunders thro'.

NATURE! great Parent! whose directing Hand
Rolls round the Seasons of the changeful Year,
145   How mighty! how majestick are thy Works!
With what a pleasing Dread they swell the Soul,
That sees, astonish'd! and, astonish'd sings!

You too, ye *Winds!* that now begin to blow,
With boisterous Sweep, I raise my Voice to you.
150 Where are your Stores, ye viewless *Beings!* say?
Where your aerial Magazines reserv'd,
Against the Day of Tempest perilous?
In what untravel'd Country of the Air,
Hush'd in still Silence, sleep you, when 'tis calm?

155 LATE, in the louring Sky, red, fiery, Streaks
Begin to flush about; the reeling Clouds
Stagger with dizzy Aim, as doubting yet
Which Master to obey: while rising, slow.
Sad, in the Leaden-colour'd East, the Moon
160 Wears a bleak Circle round her sully'd Orb.
Then issues forth the Storm, with loud Control,
And the thin Fabrick of the pillar'd Air
O'erturns, at once. Prone, on th' uncertain Main,
Descends th' Etherial Force, and plows its Waves,
165 With dreadful Rift: from the mid-Deep, appears,
Surge after Surge, the rising, wat'ry, War.
Whitening, the angry Billows rowl immense,
And roar their Terrors, through the shuddering Soul
Of feeble Man, amidst their Fury caught,
170 And, dash'd upon his Fate: Then, o'er the Cliff,
Where dwells the *Sea-Mew,* unconfin'd, they fly,
And, hurrying, swallow up the steril Shore.

THE Mountain growls; and all its sturdy *Sons*
Stoop to the Bottom of the Rocks they shade:
175 Lone, on its Midnight-Side, and all aghast,
The dark, way-faring, *Stranger,* breathless, toils,
And climbs against the Blast—
Low, waves the rooted Forest, vex'd, and sheds
What of its leafy Honours yet remains.
180 Thus, struggling thro' the dissipated Grove,
The whirling Tempest raves along the Plain;
And, on the Cottage thacht, or lordly Dome,
Keen-fastening, shakes 'em to the solid Base.

Sleep, frighted, flies; the hollow Chimney howls,
185 The Windows rattle, and the Hinges creak.

THEN, too, they say, thro' all the burthen'd Air,
Long Groans are heard, shrill Sounds, and distant Sighs.
That, murmur'd by the *Demon* of the Night,
Warn the devoted *Wretch* of Woe, and Death!
190 Wild Uproar lords it wide: the Clouds commixt,
With Stars, swift-gliding, sweep along the Sky.
All Nature reels.—But hark! The *Almighty* speaks:
Instant, the chidden Storm begins to pant,
And dies, at once, into a noiseless Calm.

195 AS yet, 'tis Midnight's Reign; the weary Clouds,
Slow-meeting, mingle into solid Gloom:
Now, while the drousy World lies lost in Sleep,
Let me associate with the low-brow'd *Night,*
And *Contemplation,* her sedate Compeer;
200 Let me shake off th' intrusive Cares of Day,
And lay the medling Senses all aside.

AND now, ye lying *Vanities* of Life!
You ever-tempting, ever-cheating Train!
Where are you now? and what is your Amount?
205 Vexation, Disappointment, and Remorse.
Sad, sickening, Thought! and yet, deluded Man,
A Scene of wild, disjointed, Visions past,
And broken Slumbers, rises, still resolv'd,
With new-flush'd Hopes, to run your giddy Round.

210 FATHER of Light, and Life! Thou *Good Supreme!*
O! teach me what is Good! teach me thy self!
Save me from Folly, Vanity and Vice,
From every low Pursuit! and feed my Soul,
With Knowledge, conscious Peace, and Vertue pure,
215 Sacred, substantial, never-fading Bliss!

LO! from the livid East, or piercing North,
Thick Clouds ascend, in whose capacious Womb,

A vapoury Deluge lies, to Snow congeal'd:
Heavy, they roll their fleecy World along;
220 And the Sky saddens with th' impending Storm.
Thro' the hush'd Air, the whitening Shower descends,
At first, thin-wavering; till, at last, the Flakes
Fall broad, and wide, and fast, dimming the Day,
With a continual Flow. See! sudden, hoar'd,
225 The Woods beneath the stainless Burden bow,
Blackning, along the mazy Stream it melts;
Earth's universal Face, deep-hid, and chill,
Is all one, dazzling, Waste. The Labourer-Ox
Stands cover'd o'er with Snow, and then demands
230 The Fruit of all his Toil. The Fowls of Heaven,
Tam'd by the cruel Season, croud around
The winnowing Store, and claim the little Boon,
That *Providence* allows. The foodless Wilds
Pour forth their brown *Inhabitants;* the Hare,
235 Tho' timorous of Heart, and hard beset
By Death, in various Forms, dark Snares, and Dogs,
And more unpitying Men, the Garden seeks,
Urg'd on by *fearless* Want. The bleating Kind
Eye the bleak Heavens, and next, the glistening Earth,
240 With Looks of dumb Despair; then sad, dispers'd,
Dig, for the wither'd Herb, thro' Heaps of Snow.

NOW, *Shepherds,* to your helpless Charge be kind;
Baffle the raging Year, and fill their Penns
With Food, at will: lodge them below the Blast,
245 And watch them strict; for from the bellowing East,
In this dire Season, oft the Whirlwind's Wing
Sweeps up the Burthen of whole wintry Plains,
In one fierce Blast, and o'er th' unhappy Flocks,
Lodged in the Hollow of two neighbouring Hills,
250 The billowy Tempest whelms; till, upwards urg'd,
The Valley to a shining Mountain swells,
That curls its Wreaths amid the freezing Sky.

NOW, all amid the Rigours of the Year,

In the wild Depth of Winter, while without
255   The ceaseless Winds blow keen, be my Retreat
A rural, shelter'd, solitary, Scene;
Where ruddy Fire, and beaming Tapers join
To chase the chearless Gloom: there let me sit,
And hold high Converse with the mighty Dead,
260   *Sages* of ancient Time, as Gods rever'd,
As Gods beneficent, who blest Mankind,
With Arts, and Arms, and humaniz'd a World.
Rous'd at th' inspiring Thought—I throw aside
The long-liv'd Volume, and, deep-musing, hail
265   The sacred *Shades,* that, slowly-rising, pass
Before my wondering Eyes—First, *Socrates,*
Truth's early Champion, Martyr for his God:
Solon, the next, who built his Commonweal,
On Equity's firm Base: *Lycurgus,* then,
270   Severely good, and him of rugged *Rome,*
Numa, who soften'd *her* rapacious *Sons.*
Cimon, sweet-soul'd, and *Aristides* just.
Unconquer'd *Cato,* virtuous in Extreme;
With that attemper'd *Heroe, mild, and firm,
275   Who wept the Brother, while the Tyrant bled.
Scipio, the humane Warriour, gently brave,
Fair Learning's Friend; who early sought the Shade,
To dwell, with *Innocence,* and *Truth,* retir'd.
And, equal to the best, the *Theban, He*
280   Who, *single,* rais'd his Country into Fame.
Thousands behind, the Boast of *Greece* and *Rome,*
Whom *Vertue* owns, the Tribute of a Verse
Demand, but who can count the Stars of Heaven?
Who sing their Influence on this lower World?
285   But see who yonder comes! nor comes alone,
With *sober* State, and of *majestic* Mien,
The Sister-Muses in his Train—'Tis He!
Maro! the best of Poets, and of Men!

* *Timoleon.*

Great *Homer* too appears, of *daring* Wing!
290 *Parent* of Song! and *equal,* by his Side,
The *British Muse,* join'd Hand in Hand, they walk,
Darkling, nor miss their Way to Fame's Ascent.
Society divine! Immortal Minds!
Still visit thus my Nights, for *you* reserv'd,
295 And mount my soaring Soul to Deeds like yours.
Silence! thou lonely *Power!* the Door be thine:
See, on the hallow'd Hour, that none intrude,
Save *Lycidas,* the Friend, with Sense refin'd,
Learning digested well, exalted Faith,
300 Unstudy'd Wit, and Humour ever gay.

CLEAR Frost succeeds, and thro' the blew Serene,
For Sight too fine, th' Ætherial Nitre flies,
To bake the Glebe, and bind the slip'ry Flood.
This of the wintry Season is the Prime;
305 Pure are the Days, and lustrous are the Nights,
Brighten'd with starry Worlds, till then unseen.
Mean while, the Orient, darkly red, breathes forth
An Icy Gale, that, in its mid Career,
Arrests the bickering Stream. The nightly Sky,
310 And all her glowing Constellations pour
Their rigid Influence down: It freezes on
Till Morn, late-rising, o'er the drooping World,
Lifts her pale Eye, unjoyous: then appears
The various Labour of the silent Night,
315 The pendant Isicle, the Frost-Work fair,
Where thousand Figures rise, the crusted Snow,
Tho' white, made whiter, by the fining North.
On blithsome Frolic bent, the youthful Swains,
While every Work of Man is laid at Rest,
320 Rush o'er the watry Plains, and, shuddering, view
The fearful Deeps below: or with the Gun,
And faithful Spaniel, range the ravag'd Fields,
And, adding to the Ruins of the Year,
Distress the Feathery, or the Footed *Game.*

325   BUT hark! the nightly Winds, with hollow Voice,
      Blow, blustering, from the South—the Frost subdu'd,
      Gradual, resolves into a weeping Thaw.
      Spotted, the Mountains shine: loose Sleet descends,
      And floods the Country round: the Rivers swell,
330   Impatient for the Day.—Those sullen Seas,
      That wash th' ungenial Pole, will rest no more,
      Beneath the Shackles of the mighty North;
      But, rousing all their Waves, resistless heave,—
      And hark!—the length'ning Roar, continuous, runs
335   Athwart the rifted Main; at once, it bursts,
      And piles a thousand Mountains to the Clouds!
      Ill fares the Bark, the Wretches' last Resort,
      That, lost amid the floating Fragments, moors
      Beneath the Shelter of an Icy Isle;
340   While Night o'erwhelms the Sea, and Horror looks
      More horrible. Can human Hearts endure
      Th' assembled *Mischiefs,* that besiege them round:
      Unlist'ning *Hunger,* fainting *Weariness,*
      The *Roar* of Winds, and Waves, the *Crush* of Ice,
345   Now, ceasing, now, renew'd, with louder Rage,
      And bellowing round the Main: Nations remote,
      Shook from their Midnight-Slumbers, deem they hear
      Portentous Thunder, in the troubled Sky.
      More to embroil the Deep, Leviathan,
350   And his unweildy Train, in horrid Sport,
      Tempest the loosen'd Brine; while, thro' the Gloom,
      Far, from the dire, unhospitable Shore,
      The Lyon's Rage, the Wolf's sad Howl is heard,
      And all the fell Society of Night.
355   Yet, *Providence,* that ever-waking *Eye*
      Looks down, with Pity, on the fruitless Toil
      Of Mortals, lost to Hope, and *lights* them safe,
      Thro' all this dreary Labyrinth of Fate.

      'TIS done!—Dread WINTER has subdued the Year,
360   And reigns, tremenduous, o'er the desart Plains!
      How dead the Vegetable Kingdom lies!

How dumb the Tuneful! *Horror* wide extends
His solitary Empire.—Now, fond *Man!*
Behold thy pictur'd life: Pass some few Years,
365 Thy flow'ring SPRING, Thy short-liv'd SUMMER's Strength,
Thy sober AUTUMN, fading into Age,
And pale, concluding, WINTER shuts thy Scene,
And shrouds *Thee* in the Grave—where now, are fled
Those Dreams of Greatness? those unsolid Hopes
370 Of Happiness? those Longings after Fame?
Those restless Cares? those busy, bustling Days?
Those Nights of secret Guilt? those veering Thoughts,
Flutt'ring 'twixt Good, and Ill, that shar'd thy Life?
All, now, are vanish'd! *Vertue,* sole, survives,
375 Immortal, Mankind's never-failing Friend,
His Guide to Happiness on high—and see!
'Tis come, the Glorious *Morn!* the second Birth
Of Heaven, and Earth!—awakening *Nature* hears
Th' Almighty Trumpet's Voice, and starts to Life,
380 Renew'd, unfading. Now, th' Eternal *Scheme,*
That Dark Perplexity, that Mystic Maze,
Which Sight cou'd never trace, nor Heart conceive,
To *Reason's* Eye, refin'd, clears up apace.
Angels, and Men, astonish'd, pause—and dread
385 To travel thro' the Depths of Providence,
Untry'd, unbounded. Ye vain *Learned!* see,
And, prostrate in the Dust, adore that *Power,*
And *Goodness,* oft arraign'd. See now the Cause,
Why conscious *Worth,* oppress'd, in secret long
390 Mourn'd, unregarded: Why the *Good Man's* Sha[re]
In Life, was Gall, and Bitterness of Soul:
Why the lone *Widow,* and her *Orphans,* pin'd,
In starving Solitude; while *Luxury,*
In Palaces, lay prompting her low Thought,
395 To form unreal Wants: why Heaven-born *Faith,*
And *Charity,* prime Grace! wore the *red* Marks
Of *Persecution's* Scourge: Why licens'd *Pain,*
That cruel *Spoiler,* that embosom'd *Foe,*

51

Imbitter'd all our Bliss. Ye Good *Distrest!*
400 Ye Noble *Few!* that, here, unbending, stand
Beneath Life's Pressures—yet a little while,
And all your Woes are past. *Time* swiftly fleets,
And wish'd *Eternity,* approaching, brings
Life undecaying, Love without Allay,
405 Pure flowing Joy, and Happiness sincere.

III. THE MOCK-HEROIC POEM

Alexander Pope

THE RAPE OF THE LOCK

CANTO I.

WHAT dire Offence from am'rous Causes springs,
What mighty Contests rise from trivial Things,
I sing—This Verse to *Caryll,* Muse! is due;
This, ev'n *Belinda* may vouchsafe to view:
5   Slight is the Subject, but not so the Praise,
If She inspire, and He approve my Lays.
    Say what strange Motive, Goddess! cou'd compel
A well-bred *Lord* t'assault a gentle *Belle*?
Oh say what stranger Cause, yet unexplor'd,
10   Cou'd make a gentle *Belle* reject a *Lord*?
In Tasks so bold, can Little Men engage,
And in soft Bosoms dwells such mighty Rage?
    Sol thro' white Curtains shot a tim'rous Ray,
And op'd those Eyes that must eclipse the Day;
15   Now Lapdogs give themselves the rowzing Shake,
And sleepless Lovers, just at Twelve, awake:
Thrice rung the Bell, the Slipper knock'd the Ground,
And the press'd Watch return'd a silver Sound.
Belinda still her downy Pillow prest,
20   Her Guardian *Sylph* prolong'd the balmy Rest.
'Twas he had summon'd to her silent Bed
The Morning-Dream that hover'd o'er her Head.
A Youth more glitt'ring than a *Birth-night Beau,*
(That ev'n in Slumber caus'd her Cheek to glow)
25   Seem'd to her Ear his winning Lips to lay,
And thus in Whispers said, or seem'd to say.

Fairest of Mortals, thou distinguish'd Care
Of thousand bright Inhabitants of Air!
If e'er one Vision touch'd thy infant Thought,
30 Of all the Nurse and all the Priest have taught,
Of airy Elves by Moonlight Shadows seen,
The silver Token, and the circled Green,
Or Virgins visited by Angel-Pow'rs,
With Golden Crowns and Wreaths of heav'nly Flow'rs,
35 Hear and believe! thy own Importance know,
Nor bound thy narrow Views to Things below.
Some secret Truths from Learned Pride conceal'd,
To Maids alone and Children are reveal'd:
What tho' no Credit doubting Wits may give?
40 The Fair and Innocent shall still believe.
Know then, unnumber'd Spirits round thee fly,
The light *Militia* of the lower Sky;
These, tho' unseen, are ever on the Wing,
Hang o'er the *Box,* and hover round the *Ring.*
45 Think what an Equipage thou hast in Air,
And view with scorn *Two Pages* and a *Chair.*
As now your own, our Beings were of old,
And once inclos'd in Woman's beauteous Mold;
Thence, by a soft Transition, we repair
50 From earthly Vehicles to these of Air.
Think not, when Woman's transient Breath is fled,
That all her Vanities at once are dead:
Succeeding Vanities she still regards,
And tho' she plays no more, o'erlooks the Cards.
55 Her Joy in gilded Chariots, when alive,
And Love of *Ombre,* after Death survive.
For when the Fair in all their Pride expire,
To their first Elements their Souls retire:
The Sprights of fiery Termagants in Flame
60 Mount up, and take a *Salamander's* Name.
Soft yielding Minds to Water glide away,
And sip with *Nymphs,* their Elemental Tea.
The graver Prude sinks downward to a *Gnome,*

In search of Mischief still on Earth to roam.
65 The light Coquettes in *Sylphs* aloft repair,
And sport and flutter in the Fields of Air.
    Know farther yet; Whoever fair and chaste
Rejects Mankind, is by some *Sylph* embrac'd:
For Spirits, freed from mortal Laws, with ease
70 Assume what Sexes and what Shapes they please.
What guards the Purity of melting Maids,
In Courtly Balls, and Midnight Masquerades,
Safe from the treach'rous Friend, the daring Spark,
The Glance by Day, the Whisper in the Dark;
75 When kind Occasion prompts their warm Desires,
When Musick softens, and when Dancing fires?
'Tis but their *Sylph,* the wise Celestials know,
Tho' *Honour* is the Word with Men below.
    Some Nymphs there are, too conscious of their Face,
80 For Life predestin'd to the *Gnomes'* Embrace.
These swell their Prospects and exalt their Pride,
When Offers are disdain'd, and Love deny'd.
Then gay Ideas crowd the vacant Brain;
While Peers and Dukes, and all their sweeping Train,
85 And Garters, Stars, and Coronets appear,
And in soft Sounds, *Your Grace* salutes their Ear.
'Tis these that early taint the Female Soul,
Instruct the Eyes of young *Coquettes* to roll,
Teach Infant-Cheeks a bidden Blush to know,
90 And little Hearts to flutter at a *Beau.*
    Oft when the World imagine Women stray,
The *Sylphs* thro' mystick Mazes guide their Way,
Thro' all the giddy Circle they pursue,
And old Impertinence expel by new.
95 What tender Maid but must a Victim fall
To one Man's Treat, but for another's Ball?
When *Florio* speaks, what Virgin could withstand,
If gentle *Damon* did not squeeze her Hand?
With varying Vanities, from ev'ry Part,
100 They shift the moving Toyshop of their Heart;

Where Wigs with Wigs, with Sword-knots Sword-knots strive,
Beaus banish Beaus, and Coaches Coaches drive.
This erring Mortals Levity may call,
Oh blind to Truth! the *Sylphs* contrive it all.
105   Of these am I, who thy Protection claim,
A watchful Sprite, and *Ariel* is my Name.
Late, as I rang'd the Crystal Wilds of Air,
In the clear Mirror of thy ruling *Star*
I saw, alas! some dread Event impend,
110   Ere to the Main this Morning Sun descend.
But Heav'n reveals not what, or how, or where:
Warn'd by thy *Sylph,* oh Pious Maid beware!
This to disclose is all thy Guardian can.
Beware of all, but most beware of Man!
115   He said; when *Shock,* who thought she slept too long,
Leapt up, and wak'd his Mistress with his Tongue.
'Twas then *Belinda!* if Report say true,
Thy Eyes first open'd on a *Billet-doux;*
Wounds, Charms, and *Ardors,* were no sooner read,
120   But all the Vision vanish'd from thy Head.
    And now, unveil'd, the *Toilet* stands display'd,
Each Silver Vase in mystic Order laid.
First, rob'd in White, the Nymph intent adores
With Head uncover'd, the *Cosmetic* Pow'rs.
125   A heav'nly Image in the Glass appears,
To that she bends, to that her Eyes she rears;
Th'inferior Priestess, at her Altar's side,
Trembling, begins the sacred Rites of Pride.
Unnumber'd Treasures ope at once, and here
130   The various Off'rings of the World appear;
From each she nicely culls with curious Toil,
And decks the Goddess with the glitt'ring Spoil.
This Casket *India's* glowing Gems unlocks,
And all *Arabia* breathes from yonder Box.
135   The Tortoise here and Elephant unite,
Transform'd to *Combs,* the speckled and the white.
Here Files of Pins extend their shining Rows,

Puffs, Powders, Patches, Bibles, Billet-doux.
Now awful Beauty puts on all its Arms;
140 The Fair each moment rises in her Charms,
Repairs her Smiles, awakens ev'ry Grace,
And calls forth all the Wonders of her Face;
Sees by Degrees a purer Blush arise,
And keener Lightnings quicken in her Eyes.
145 The busy *Sylphs* surround their darling Care;
These set the Head, and those divide the Hair,
Some fold the Sleeve, whilst others plait the Gown;
And *Betty's* prais'd for Labours not her own.

CANTO II.

NOT with more Glories, in th' Etherial Plain,
The Sun first rises o'er the purpled Main,
Than issuing forth, the Rival of his Beams
Launch'd on the Bosom of the Silver *Thames.*
5 Fair Nymphs, and well-drest Youths around her shone,
But ev'ry Eye was fix'd on her alone.
On her white Breast a sparkling *Cross* she wore,
Which *Jews* might kiss, and Infidels adore.
Her lively Looks a sprightly Mind disclose,
10 Quick as her Eyes, and as unfix'd as those:
Favours to none, to all she Smiles extends,
Oft she rejects, but never once offends.
Bright as the Sun, her Eyes the Gazers strike,
And, like the Sun, they shine on all alike.
15 Yet graceful Ease, and Sweetness void of Pride,
Might hide her Faults, if *Belles* had Faults to hide:
If to her share some Female Errors fall,
Look on her Face, and you'll forget 'em all.
     This Nymph, to the Destruction of Mankind,
20 Nourish'd two Locks, which graceful hung behind
In equal Curls, and well conspir'd to deck
With shining Ringlets the smooth Iv'ry Neck.
Love in these Labyrinths his Slaves detains,
And mighty Hearts are held in slender Chains.

25   With hairy Sprindges we the Birds betray,
       Slight Lines of Hair surprize the Finny Prey,
       Fair Tresses Man's Imperial Race insnare,
       And Beauty draws us with a single Hair.
           Th' Adventrous *Baron* the bright Locks admir'd,
30   He saw, he wish'd, and to the Prize aspir'd:
       Resolv'd to win, he meditates the way,
       By Force to ravish, or by Fraud betray;
       For when Success a Lover's Toil attends,
       Few ask, if Fraud or Force attain'd his Ends.
35   For this, ere *Phœbus* rose, he had implor'd
       Propitious Heav'n, and ev'ry Pow'r ador'd,
       But chiefly *Love*—to *Love* an Altar built,
       Of twelve vast *French* Romances, neatly gilt.
       There lay three Garters, half a Pair of Gloves;
40   And all the Trophies of his former Loves.
       With tender *Billet-doux* he lights the Pyre,
       And breathes three am'rous Sighs to raise the Fire.
       Then prostrate falls, and begs with ardent Eyes
       Soon to obtain, and long possess the Prize:
45   The Pow'rs gave Ear, and granted half his Pray'r,
       The rest, the Winds dispers'd in empty Air.
           But now secure the painted Vessel glides,
       The Sun-beams trembling on the floating Tydes,
       While melting Musick steals upon the Sky,
50   And soften'd Sounds along the Waters die.
       Smooth flow the Waves, the Zephyrs gently play,
       Belinda smil'd, and all the World was gay.
       All but the *Sylph*—With careful Thoughts opprest,
       Th'impending Woe sate heavy on his Breast.
55   He summons strait his Denizens of Air;
       The lucid Squadrons round the Sails repair:
       Soft o'er the Shrouds Aerial Whispers breathe,
       That seem'd but *Zephyrs* to the Train beneath.
       Some to the Sun their Insect-Wings unfold,
60   Waft on the Breeze, or sink in Clouds of Gold.
       Transparent Forms, too fine for mortal Sight,

Their fluid Bodies half dissolv'd in Light.
Loose to the Wind their airy Garments flew,
Thin glitt'ring Textures of the filmy Dew;
65 Dipt in the richest Tincture of the Skies,
Where Light disports in ever-mingling Dies,
While ev'ry Beam new transient Colours flings,
Colours that change whene'er they wave their Wings.
Amid the Circle, on the gilded Mast,
70 Superior by the Head, was *Ariel* plac'd;
His Purple Pinions opening to the Sun,
He rais'd his Azure Wand, and thus begun.
   Ye *Sylphs* and *Sylphids,* to your Chief give Ear,
Fays, Fairies, Genii, Elves, and *Dæmons* hear!
75 Ye know the Spheres and various Tasks assign'd,
By Laws Eternal, to th' Aerial Kind.
Some in the Fields of purest *Æther* play,
And bask and whiten in the Blaze of Day.
Some guide the Course of wandring Orbs on high,
80 Or roll the Planets thro' the boundless Sky.
Some less refin'd, beneath the Moon's pale Light
Pursue the Stars that shoot athwart the Night,
Or suck the Mists in grosser Air below,
Or dip their Pinions in the painted Bow,
85 Or brew fierce Tempests on the wintry Main,
Or o'er the Glebe distill the kindly Rain.
Others on Earth o'er human Race preside,
Watch all their Ways, and all their Actions guide:
Of these the Chief the Care of Nations own,
90 And guard with Arms Divine the *British Throne.*
   Our humbler Province is to tend the Fair,
Not a less pleasing, tho' less glorious Care.
To save the Powder from too rude a Gale,
Nor let th' imprison'd Essences exhale,
95 To draw fresh Colours from the vernal Flow'rs,
To steal from Rainbows ere they drop in Show'rs
A brighter Wash; to curl their waving Hairs,
Assist their Blushes, and inspire their Airs;

Nay oft, in Dreams, Invention we bestow,
100 To change a *Flounce,* or add a *Furbelo.*
　　This Day, black Omens threat the brightest Fair
That e'er deserv'd a watchful Spirit's Care;
Some dire Disaster, or by Force, or Slight,
But what, or where, the Fates have wrapt in Night.
105 Whether the Nymph shall break *Diana'*s Law,
Or some frail *China* Jar receive a Flaw,
Or stain her Honour, or her new Brocade,
Forget her Pray'rs, or miss a Masquerade,
Or lose her Heart, or Necklace, at a Ball;
110 Or whether Heav'n has doom'd that *Shock* must fall.
Haste then ye Spirits! to your Charge repair;
The flutt'ring Fan be *Zephyretta'*s Care;
The Drops to thee, *Brillante,* we consign;
And, *Momentilla,* let the Watch be thine;
115 Do thou, *Crispissa,* tend her fav'rite Lock;
Ariel himself shall be the Guard of *Shock.*
　　To Fifty chosen *Sylphs,* of special Note,
We trust th'important Charge, the *Petticoat:*
Oft have we known that sev'nfold Fence to fail,
120 Tho' stiff with Hoops, and arm'd with Ribs of Whale.
Form a strong Line about the Silver Bound,
And guard the wide Circumference around.
　　Whatever Spirit, careless of his Charge,
His Post neglects, or leaves the Fair at large,
125 Shall feel sharp Vengeance soon o'ertake his Sins,
Be stopt in *Vials,* or transfixt with *Pins;*
Or plung'd in Lakes of bitter *Washes* lie,
Or wedg'd whole Ages in a *Bodkin'*s Eye:
Gums and *Pomatums* shall his Flight restrain,
130 While clog'd he beats his silken Wings in vain;
Or Alom-*Stypticks* with contracting Power
Shrink his thin Essence like a rivell'd Flower.
Or as *Ixion* fix'd, the Wretch shall feel
The giddy Motion of the whirling Mill,
135 In Fumes of burning Chocolate shall glow,

And tremble at the Sea that froaths below!
　　He spoke; the Spirits from the Sails descend;
Some, Orb in Orb, around the Nymph extend,
Some thrid the mazy Ringlets of her Hair,
140　Some hang upon the Pendants of her Ear;
With beating Hearts the dire Event they wait,
Anxious, and trembling for the Birth of Fate.

CANTO III.

CLOSE by those Meads for ever crown'd with Flow'rs,
Where *Thames* with Pride surveys his rising Tow'rs,
There stands a Structure of Majestick Frame,
Which from the neighb'ring *Hampton* takes its Name.
5　Here *Britain's* Statesmen oft the Fall foredoom
Of Foreign Tyrants, and of Nymphs at home;
Here Thou, Great *Anna!* whom three Realms obey,
Dost sometimes Counsel take—and sometimes *Tea.*
　　Hither the Heroes and the Nymphs resort,
10　To taste awhile the Pleasures of a Court;
In various Talk th'instructive hours they past,
Who gave the *Ball,* or paid the *Visit* last:
One speaks the Glory of the *British Queen,*
And one describes a charming *Indian Screen;*
15　A third interprets Motions, Looks, and Eyes;
At ev'ry Word a Reputation dies.
Snuff, or the *Fan,* supply each Pause of Chat,
With singing, laughing, ogling, and all that.
　　Mean while declining from the Noon of Day,
20　The Sun obliquely shoots his burning Ray;
The hungry Judges soon the Sentence sign,
And Wretches hang that Jury-men may Dine;
The Merchant from th'*Exchange* returns in Peace,
And the long Labours of the *Toilette* cease—
25　*Belinda* now, whom Thirst of Fame invites,
Burns to encounter two adventrous Knights,
At *Ombre* singly to decide their Doom;

And swells her Breast with Conquests yet to come.
Strait the three Bands prepare in Arms to join,
30   Each Band the number of the Sacred Nine.
Soon as she spreads her Hand, th' Aerial Guard
Descend, and sit on each important Card:
First *Ariel* perch'd upon a *Matadore*,
Then each, according to the Rank they bore;
35   For *Sylphs,* yet mindful of their ancient Race,
Are, as when Women, wondrous fond of Place.
      Behold, four *Kings* in Majesty rever'd,
With hoary Whiskers and a forky Beard;
And four fair *Queens* whose hands sustain a Flow'r,
40   Th' expressive Emblem of their softer Pow'r;
Four *Knaves* in Garbs succinct, a trusty Band,
Caps on their heads, and Halberds in their hand;
And Particolour'd Troops, a shining Train,
Draw forth to Combat on the Velvet Plain.
45   The skilful Nymph reviews her Force with Care;
Let Spades be Trumps! she said, and Trumps they were.
      Now move to War her Sable *Matadores,*
In Show like Leaders of the swarthy *Moors.*
Spadillio first, unconquerable Lord!
50   Led off two captive Trumps, and swept the Board.
As many more *Manillio* forc'd to yield,
And march'd a Victor from the verdant Field.
Him *Basto* follow'd, but his Fate more hard
Gain'd but one Trump and one *Plebeian* Card.
55   With his broad Sabre next, a Chief in Years,
The hoary Majesty of *Spades* appears;
Puts forth one manly Leg, to sight reveal'd;
The rest his many-colour'd Robe conceal'd.
The Rebel-*Knave,* who dares his Prince engage,
60   Proves the just Victim of his Royal Rage.
Ev'n mighty *Pam* that Kings and Queens o'erthrew,
And mow'd down Armies in the Fights of *Lu.*
Sad Chance of War! now, destitute of Aid,
Falls undistinguish'd by the Victor *Spade!*

65   Thus far both Armies to *Belinda* yield;
        Now to the *Baron* Fate inclines the Field.
        His warlike *Amazon* her Host invades,
        Th' Imperial Consort of the Crown of *Spades.*
        The *Club*'s black Tyrant first her Victim dy'd,
70   Spite of his haughty Mien, and barb'rous Pride:
        What boots the Regal Circle on his Head,
        His Giant Limbs in State unwieldy spread?
        That long behind he trails his pompous Robe,
        And of all Monarchs only grasps the Globe?
75   The *Baron* now his *Diamonds* pours apace;
        Th' embroider'd *King* who shows but half his Face,
        And his refulgent *Queen,* with Pow'rs combin'd,
        Of broken Troops an easie Conquest find.
        Clubs, Diamonds, Hearts, in wild Disorder seen,
80   With Throngs promiscuous strow the level Green.
        Thus when dispers'd a routed Army runs,
        Of *Asia*'s Troops, and *Africk*'s Sable Sons,
        With like Confusion different Nations fly,
        Of various Habit and of various Dye,
85   The pierc'd Battalions dis-united fall,
        In Heaps on Heaps; one Fate o'erwhelms them all.
          The *Knave* of *Diamonds* tries his wily Arts,
        And wins (oh shameful Chance!) the *Queen* of *Hearts.*
        At this, the Blood the Virgin's Cheek forsook,
90   A livid Paleness spreads o'er all her Look;
        She sees, and trembles at th' approaching Ill,
        Just in the Jaws of Ruin, and *Codille.*
        And now, (as oft in some distemper'd State)
        On one nice *Trick* depends the gen'ral Fate.
95   An *Ace* of Hearts steps forth: The *King* unseen
        Lurk'd in her Hand, and mourn'd his captive *Queen.*
        He springs to Vengeance with an eager pace,
        And falls like Thunder on the prostrate *Ace.*
        The Nymph exulting fills with Shouts the Sky,
100   The Walls, the Woods, and long Canals reply.
          Oh thoughtless Mortals! ever blind to Fate,

Too soon dejected, and too soon elate!
Sudden these Honours shall be snatch'd away,
And curs'd for ever this Victorious Day.
105   For lo! the Board with Cups and Spoons is crown'd,
The Berries crackle, and the Mill turns round.
On shining Altars of *Japan* they raise
The silver Lamp; the fiery Spirits blaze.
From silver Spouts the grateful Liquors glide,
110 While *China*'s Earth receives the smoking Tyde.
At once they gratify their Scent and Taste,
And frequent Cups prolong the rich Repast.
Strait hover round the Fair her Airy Band;
Some, as she sip'd, the fuming Liquor fann'd,
115 Some o'er her Lap their careful Plumes display'd,
Trembling, and conscious of the rich Brocade.
Coffee, (which makes the Politician wise,
And see thro' all things with his half-shut Eyes)
Sent up in Vapours to the *Baron*'s Brain
120 New Stratagems, the radiant Lock to gain.
Ah cease rash Youth! desist ere 'tis too late,
Fear the just Gods, and think of *Scylla*'s Fate!
Chang'd to a Bird, and sent to flit in Air,
She dearly pays for *Nisus'* injur'd Hair!
125   But when to Mischief Mortals bend their Will,
How soon they find fit Instruments of Ill!
Just then, *Clarissa* drew with tempting Grace
A two-edg'd Weapon from her shining Case;
So Ladies in Romance assist their Knight,
130 Present the Spear, and arm him for the Fight.
He takes the Gift with rev'rence, and extends
The little Engine on his Fingers' Ends,
This just behind *Belinda*'s Neck he spread,
As o'er the fragrant Steams she bends her Head:
135 Swift to the Lock a thousand Sprights repair,
A thousand Wings, by turns, blow back the Hair,
And thrice they twitch'd the Diamond in her Ear,
Thrice she look'd back, and thrice the Foe drew near.

Just in that instant, anxious *Ariel* sought
140 The close Recesses of the Virgin's Thought;
As on the Nosegay in her Breast reclin'd,
He watch'd th' Ideas rising in her Mind,
Sudden he view'd, in spite of all her Art,
An Earthly Lover lurking at her Heart.
145 Amaz'd, confus'd, he found his Pow'r expir'd,
Resign'd to Fate, and with a Sigh retir'd.
      The Peer now spreads the glitt'ring *Forfex* wide,
T'inclose the Lock; now joins it, to divide.
Ev'n then, before the fatal Engine clos'd,
150 A wretched *Sylph* too fondly interpos'd;
Fate urg'd the Sheers, and cut the *Sylph* in twain,
(But Airy Substance soon unites again)
The meeting Points the sacred Hair dissever
From the fair Head, for ever and for ever!
155   Then flash'd the living Lightning from her Eyes,
And Screams of Horror rend th' affrighted Skies.
Not louder Shrieks to pitying Heav'n are cast,
When Husbands or when Lap-dogs breathe their last,
Or when rich *China* Vessels, fal'n from high,
160 In glittring Dust and painted Fragments lie!
      Let Wreaths of Triumph now my Temples twine,
(The Victor cry'd) the glorious Prize is mine!
While Fish in Streams, or Birds delight in Air,
Or in a Coach and Six the *British* Fair,
165 As long as *Atalantis* shall be read,
Or the small Pillow grace a Lady's Bed,
While *Visits* shall be paid on solemn Days,
When numerous Wax-lights in bright Order blaze,
While Nymphs take Treats, or Assignations give,
170 So long my Honour, Name, and Praise shall live!
      What Time wou'd spare, from Steel receives its date,
And Monuments, like Men, submit to Fate!
Steel cou'd the Labour of the Gods destroy,
And strike to Dust th' Imperial Tow'rs of *Troy;*
175 Steel cou'd the Works of mortal Pride confound,

And hew Triumphal Arches to the Ground.
What Wonder then, fair Nymph! thy Hairs shou'd feel
The conqu'ring Force of unresisted Steel?

CANTO IV.

BUT anxious Cares the pensive Nymph opprest,
And secret Passions labour'd in her Breast.
Not youthful Kings in Battel seiz'd alive,
Not scornful Virgins who their Charms survive,
5   Not ardent Lovers robb'd of all their Bliss,
Not ancient Ladies when refus'd a Kiss,
Not Tyrants fierce that unrepenting die,
Not *Cynthia* when her *Manteau's* pinn'd awry,
E'er felt such Rage, Resentment and Despair,
10 As Thou, sad Virgin! for thy ravish'd Hair.
    For, that sad moment, when the *Sylphs* withdrew,
And *Ariel* weeping from *Belinda* flew,
Umbriel, a dusky melancholy Spright,
As ever sully'd the fair face of Light,
15 Down to the Central Earth, his proper Scene,
Repair'd to search the gloomy Cave of *Spleen.*
    Swift on his sooty Pinions flitts the *Gnome,*
And in a Vapour reach'd the dismal Dome.
No cheerful Breeze this sullen Region knows,
20 The dreaded *East* is all the Wind that blows.
Here, in a Grotto, sheltred close from Air,
And screen'd in Shades from Day's detested Glare,
She sighs for ever on her pensive Bed,
Pain at her Side, and *Megrim* at her Head.
25   Two Handmaids wait the Throne: Alike in Place,
But diff'ring far in Figure and in Face.
Here stood *Ill-nature* like an *ancient Maid,*
Her wrinkled Form in *Black* and *White* array'd;
With store of Pray'rs, for Mornings, Nights, and Noons,
30 Her Hand is fill'd; her Bosom with Lampoons.
    There *Affectation* with a sickly Mien

Shows in her Cheek the Roses of Eighteen,
Practis'd to Lisp, and hang the Head aside,
Faints into Airs, and languishes with Pride;
35   On the rich Quilt sinks with becoming Woe,
Wrapt in a Gown, for Sickness, and for Show.
The Fair-ones feel such Maladies as these,
When each new Night-Dress gives a new Disease.
    A constant *Vapour* o'er the Palace flies;
40   Strange Phantoms rising as the Mists arise;
Dreadful, as Hermit's Dreams in haunted Shades,
Or bright as Visions of expiring Maids.
Now glaring Fiends, and Snakes on rolling Spires,
Pale Spectres, gaping Tombs, and Purple Fires:
45   Now Lakes of liquid Gold, *Elysian* Scenes,
And Crystal Domes, and Angels in Machines.
    Unnumber'd Throngs on ev'ry side are seen
Of Bodies chang'd to various Forms by *Spleen.*
Here living *Teapots* stand, one Arm held out,
50   One bent; the Handle this, and that the Spout:
A Pipkin there like *Homer's Tripod* walks;
Here sighs a Jar, and there a Goose-pye talks;
Men prove with Child, as pow'rful Fancy works,
And Maids turn'd Bottels, call aloud for Corks.
55   Safe past the *Gnome* thro' this fantastick Band,
A Branch of healing *Spleenwort* in his hand.
Then thus addrest the Pow'r—Hail wayward Queen!
Who rule the Sex to Fifty from Fifteen,
Parent of Vapors and of Female Wit,
60   Who give th' *Hysteric* or *Poetic* Fit,
On various Tempers act by various ways,
Make some take Physick, others scribble Plays;
Who cause the Proud their Visits to delay,
And send the Godly in a Pett, to pray.
65   A Nymph there is, that all thy Pow'r disdains,
And thousands more in equal Mirth maintains.
But oh! if e'er thy *Gnome* could spoil a Grace,
Or raise a Pimple on a beauteous Face,

Like Citron-Waters Matrons' Cheeks inflame,
70 Or change Complexions at a losing Game;
If e'er with airy Horns I planted Heads,
Or rumpled Petticoats, or tumbled Beds,
Or caus'd Suspicion when no Soul was rude,
Or discompos'd the Head-dress of a Prude,
75 Or e'er to costive Lap-Dog gave Disease,
Which not the Tears of brightest Eyes could ease:
Hear me, and touch *Belinda* with Chagrin;
That single Act gives half the World the Spleen.
  The Goddess with a discontented Air
80 Seems to reject him, tho' she grants his Pray'r.
A wondrous Bag with both her Hands she binds,
Like that where once *Ulysses* held the Winds;
There she collects the Force of Female Lungs,
Sighs, Sobs, and Passions, and the War of Tongues.
85 A Vial next she fills with fainting Fears,
Soft Sorrows, melting Griefs, and flowing Tears.
The *Gnome* rejoicing bears her Gifts away,
Spreads his black Wings, and slowly mounts to Day.
  Sunk in *Thalestris'* Arms the Nymph he found,
90 Her Eyes dejected and her Hair unbound.
Full o'er their Heads the swelling Bag he rent,
And all the Furies issued at the Vent.
Belinda burns with more than mortal Ire,
And fierce *Thalestris* fans the rising Fire.
95 O wretched Maid! she spread her Hands, and cry'd,
(While *Hampton*'s Ecchos, wretched Maid! reply'd)
Was it for this you took such constant Care
The *Bodkin, Comb,* and *Essence* to prepare;
For this your Locks in Paper-Durance bound,
100 For this with tort'ring Irons wreath'd around?
For this with Fillets strain'd your tender Head,
And bravely bore the double Loads of Lead?
Gods! shall the Ravisher display your Hair,
While the Fops envy, and the Ladies stare!
105 *Honour* forbid! at whose unrival'd Shrine

Ease, Pleasure, Virtue, All, our Sex resign.
Methinks already I your Tears survey,
Already hear the horrid things they say,
Already see you a degraded Toast,
110 And all your Honour in a Whisper lost!
How shall I, then, your helpless Fame defend?
'Twill then be Infamy to seem your Friend!
And shall this Prize, th' inestimable Prize,
Expos'd thro' Crystal to the gazing Eyes,
115 And heighten'd by the Diamond's circling Rays,
On that Rapacious Hand for ever blaze?
Sooner shall Grass in *Hide*-Park *Circus* grow,
And Wits take Lodgings in the Sound of *Bow;*
Sooner let Earth, Air, Sea, to *Chaos* fall,
120 Men, Monkies, Lap-dogs, Parrots, perish all!
    She said; then raging to *Sir Plume* repairs,
And bids her *Beau* demand the precious Hairs:
(*Sir Plume,* of *Amber Snuff-box* justly vain,
And the nice Conduct of a *clouded Cane*)
125 With earnest Eyes, and round unthinking Face,
He first the Snuff-box open'd, then the Case,
And thus broke out—"My Lord, why, what the Devil?
"Z—ds! damn the Lock! 'fore Gad, you must be civil!
"Plague on't! 'tis past a Jest—nay prithee, Pox!
130 "Give her the Hair"—he spoke, and rapp'd his Box.
    It grieves me much (reply'd the Peer again)
Who speaks so well shou'd ever speak in vain.
But by this Lock, this sacred Lock I swear,
(Which never more shall join its parted Hair,
135 Which never more its Honours shall renew,
Clipt from the lovely Head where late it grew)
That while my Nostrils draw the vital Air,
This Hand, which won it, shall for ever wear.
He spoke, and speaking, in proud Triumph spread
140 The long-contended Honours of her Head.
    But *Umbriel,* hateful *Gnome!* forbears not so;
He breaks the Vial whence the Sorrows flow.

Then see! the *Nymph* in beauteous Grief appears,
Her Eyes half-languishing, half-drown'd in Tears;
145 On her heav'd Bosom hung her drooping Head,
Which, with a Sigh, she rais'd; and thus she said.
    For ever curs'd be this detested Day,
Which snatch'd my best, my fav'rite Curl away!
Happy! ah ten times happy, had I been,
150 If *Hampton-Court* these Eyes had never seen!
Yet am not I the first mistaken Maid,
By Love of *Courts* to num'rous Ills betray'd.
Oh had I rather un-admir'd remain'd
In some lone Isle, or distant *Northern* Land;
155 Where the gilt *Chariot* never marks the Way,
Where none learn *Ombre,* none e'er taste *Bohea!*
There kept my Charms conceal'd from mortal Eye,
Like Roses that in Desarts bloom and die.
What mov'd my Mind with youthful Lords to rome?
160 O had I stay'd, and said my Pray'rs at home!
'Twas this, the Morning *Omens* seem'd to tell;
Thrice from my trembling hand the *Patch-box* fell;
The tott'ring *China* shook without a Wind,
Nay, *Poll* sate mute, and *Shock* was most Unkind!
165 A *Sylph* too warn'd me of the Threats of Fate,
In mystic Visions, now believ'd too late!
See the poor Remnants of these slighted Hairs!
My hands shall rend what ev'n thy Rapine spares:
These, in two sable Ringlets taught to break,
170 Once gave new Beauties to the snowie Neck.
The Sister-Lock now sits uncouth, alone,
And in its Fellow's Fate foresees its own;
Uncurl'd it hangs, the fatal Sheers demands;
And tempts once more thy sacrilegious Hands.
175 Oh hadst thou, Cruel! been content to seize
Hairs less in sight, or any Hairs but these!

SHE said: the pitying Audience melt in Tears,
But *Fate* and *Jove* had stopp'd the *Baron's* Ears.
In vain *Thalestris* with Reproach assails,
For who can move when fair *Belinda* fails?
5 Not half so fixt the *Trojan* cou'd remain,
While *Anna* begg'd and *Dido* rag'd in vain.
Then grave *Clarissa* graceful wav'd her Fan;
Silence ensu'd, and thus the Nymph began.
    Say, why are Beauties prais'd and honour'd most,
10 The wise Man's Passion, and the vain Man's Toast?
Why deck'd with all that Land and Sea afford,
Why Angels call'd, and Angel-like ador'd?
Why round our Coaches crowd the white-glov'd Beaus,
Why bows the Side-box from its inmost Rows?
15 How vain are all these Glories, all our Pains,
Unless good Sense preserve what Beauty gains:
That Men may say, when we the Front-box grace,
Behold the first in Virtue, as in Face!
Oh! if to dance all Night, and dress all Day,
20 Charm'd the Small-pox, or chas'd old Age away;
Who would not scorn what Huswife's Cares produce,
Or who would learn one earthly Thing of Use?
To patch, nay ogle, might become a Saint,
Nor could it sure be such a Sin to paint.
25 But since, alas! frail Beauty must decay,
Curl'd or uncurl'd, since Locks will turn to grey,
Since painted, or not painted, all shall fade,
And she who scorns a Man, must die a Maid;
What then remains, but well our Pow'r to use,
30 And keep good Humour still whate'er we lose?
And trust me, Dear! good Humour can prevail,
When Airs, and Flights, and Screams, and Scolding fail.
Beauties in vain their pretty Eyes may roll;
Charms strike the Sight, but Merit wins the Soul.
35   So spoke the Dame, but no Applause ensu'd;
Belinda frown'd, *Thalestris* call'd her Prude.

To Arms, to Arms! the fierce Virago cries,
And swift as Lightning to the Combate flies.
All side in Parties, and begin th' Attack;
40 Fans clap, Silks russle, and tough Whalebones crack;
Heroes' and Heroins' Shouts confus'dly rise,
And base, and treble Voices strike the Skies.
No common Weapons in their Hands are found,
Like Gods they fight, nor dread a mortal Wound.

45   So when bold *Homer* makes the Gods engage,
And heav'nly Breasts with human Passions rage;
'Gainst *Pallas, Mars; Latona, Hermes* arms;
And all *Olympus* rings with loud Alarms.
Jove's Thunder roars, Heav'n trembles all around;
50 Blue *Neptune* storms, the bellowing Deeps resound;
Earth shakes her nodding Tow'rs, the Ground gives way;
And the pale Ghosts start at the Flash of Day!
      Triumphant *Umbriel* on a Sconce's Height
Clapt his glad Wings, and sate to view the Fight:
55 Propt on their Bodkin Spears, the Sprights survey
The growing Combat, or assist the Fray.
      While thro' the Press enrag'd *Thalestris* flies,
And scatters Deaths around from both her Eyes,
A *Beau* and *Witling* perish'd in the Throng,
60 One dy'd in *Metaphor,* and one in *Song.*
O cruel Nymph! a living Death I bear,
Cry'd *Dapperwit,* and sunk beside his Chair.
A mournful Glance Sir *Fopling* upwards cast,
Those Eyes are made so killing—was his last:
65 Thus on *Meander*'s flow'ry Margin lies
Th' expiring Swan, and as he sings he dies.
      When bold Sir *Plume* had drawn *Clarissa* down,
Chloe stept in, and kill'd him with a Frown;
She smil'd to see the doughty Hero slain,
70 But at her Smile, the Beau reviv'd again.
      Now *Jove* suspends his golden Scales in Air,
Weighs the Men's Wits against the Lady's Hair;
The doubtful Beam long nods from side to side;

At length the Wits mount up, the Hairs subside.

75   See fierce *Belinda* on the *Baron* flies,
With more than usual Lightning in her Eyes;
Nor fear'd the Chief th'unequal Fight to try,
Who sought no more than on his Foe to die.
But this bold Lord, with manly Strength indu'd,

80   She with one Finger and a Thumb subdu'd:
Just where the Breath of Life his Nostrils drew,
A Charge of *Snuff* the wily Virgin threw;
The *Gnomes* direct, to ev'ry Atome just,
The pungent Grains of titillating Dust.

85   Sudden, with starting Tears each Eye o'erflows,
And the high Dome re-ecchoes to his Nose.

     Now meet thy Fate, incens'd *Belinda* cry'd,
And drew a deadly *Bodkin* from her Side.
(The same, his ancient Personage to deck,

90   Her great great Grandsire wore about his Neck
In three *Seal-Rings;* which after, melted down,
Form'd a vast *Buckle* for his Widow's Gown:
Her infant Grandame's *Whistle* next it grew,
The *Bells* she gingled, and the *Whistle* blew;

95   Then in a *Bodkin* grac'd her Mother's Hairs,
Which long she wore, and now *Belinda* wears.)

     Boast not my Fall (he cry'd) insulting Foe!
Thou by some other shalt be laid as low.
Nor think, to die dejects my lofty Mind;

100 All that I dread, is leaving you behind!
Rather than so, ah let me still survive,
And burn in *Cupid's* Flames,—but burn alive.

     Restore the Lock! she cries; and all around
Restore the Lock! the vaulted Roofs rebound.

105 Not fierce *Othello* in so loud a Strain
Roar'd for the Handkerchief that caus'd his Pain.
But see how oft Ambitious Aims are cross'd,
And Chiefs contend 'till all the Prize is lost!
The Lock, obtain'd with Guilt, and kept with Pain,

110 In ev'ry place is sought, but sought in vain:

With such a Prize no Mortal must be blest,
So Heav'n decrees! with Heav'n who can contest?
    Some thought it mounted to the Lunar Sphere,
Since all things lost on Earth, are treasur'd there.
115 There Heroes' Wits are kept in pondrous Vases,
And Beaus' in *Snuff-boxes* and *Tweezer-Cases.*
There broken Vows, and Death-bed Alms are found,
And Lovers' Hearts with Ends of Riband bound;
The Courtier's Promises, and Sick Man's Pray'rs,
120 The Smiles of Harlots, and the Tears of Heirs,
Cages for Gnats, and Chains to Yoak a Flea;
Dry'd Butterflies, and Tomes of Casuistry.
    But trust the Muse—she saw it upward rise,
Tho' mark'd by none but quick Poetic Eyes:
125 (So *Rome's* great Founder to the Heav'ns withdrew,
To *Proculus* alone confess'd in view.)
A sudden Star, it shot thro' liquid Air,
And drew behind a radiant *Trail of Hair.*
Not *Berenice's* Locks first rose so bright,
130 The Heav'ns bespangling with dishevel'd Light.
The *Sylphs* behold it kindling as it flies,
And pleas'd pursue its Progress thro' the Skies.
    This the *Beau-monde* shall from the *Mall* survey,
And hail with Musick its propitious Ray.
135 This, the blest Lover shall for *Venus* take,
And send up Vows from *Rosamonda's* Lake.
This *Partridge* soon shall view in cloudless Skies,
When next he looks thro' *Galilæo's* Eyes;
And hence th' Egregious Wizard shall foredoom
140 The Fate of *Louis,* and the Fall of *Rome.*
Then cease, bright Nymph! to mourn thy ravish'd Hair
Which adds new Glory to the shining Sphere!
Not all the Tresses that fair Head can boast
Shall draw such Envy as the Lock you lost.
145 For, after all the Murders of your Eye,
When, after Millions slain, your self shall die;
When those fair Suns shall sett, as sett they must,

And all those Tresses shall be laid in Dust;
This Lock, the Muse shall consecrate to Fame,
150 And mid'st the Stars inscribe *Belinda'*s Name!

FINIS.

IV. SATIRES

Daniel Defoe

THE TRUE-BORN ENGLISHMAN – A SATYR

('Introduction')

SPEAK, *Satyr;* for there's none can tell like thee,
Whether 'tis Folly, Pride, or Knavery,
That makes this discontented Land appear
Less happy now in Times of Peace, than War:
5   Why Civil Feuds disturb the Nation more,
Than all our Bloody Wars have done before.

   Fools out of Favour grudge at Knaves in Place,
And men are always honest in Disgrace:
The Court-Preferments make men Knaves in course:
10   But they which wou'd be in them wou'd be worse.
'Tis not at Foreigners that we repine,
Wou'd Foreigners their Perquisites resign:
The Grand Contention's plainly to be seen,
To get some men put out, and some put in.
15   For this our Senators make long Harangues.
And florid Members whet their polish'd Tongues.
Statesmen are always sick of one Disease;
And a good Pension gives them present Ease.
That's the Specifick makes them all content
20   With any King, and any Government.
Good Patriots at Court-Abuses rail,
And all the Nation's Grievances bewail:
But when the *Sov'reign Balsam's* once apply'd,
The Zealot never fails to change his Side;
25   And when he must the *Golden Key* resign,
The *Railing Spirit* comes about again.

Who shall this Bubbl'd Nation disabuse,
While they their own Felicities refuse?
Who at the Wars have made such mighty Pother,
30 And now are falling out with one another:
With needless Fears the Jealous Nation fill,
And always have been sav'd against their Will:
Who Fifty Millions *Sterling* have disburs'd,
To be with Peace and too much Plenty curs'd.
35 Who their Old Monarch eagerly undo,
And yet uneasily obey the New.
Search, *Satyr,* search, a deep Incision make;
The Poyson's strong, the Antidote's too weak.
Tis pointed Truth must manage this Dispute,
40 And down-right English *Englishmen* confute.

Whet thy just Anger at the Nation's Pride;
And with keen Phrase repel the Vicious Tide.
To *Englishmen* their own beginnings show,
And ask them why they slight their Neighbours so.
45 Go back to elder Times, and Ages past,
And Nations into long Oblivion cast;
To old *Britannia's* Youthful Days retire,
And there for *True-Born Englishmen* enquire.
Britannia freely will disown the Name,
50 And hardly knows her self from whence they came:
Wonders that They of all men shou'd pretend
To *Birth* and *Blood,* and for a Name contend.
Go back to Causes where our Follies dwell,
And fetch the dark Original from Hell:
55 Speak, *Satyr,* for there's none like thee can tell.

Jonathan Swift

A SATIRICAL ELEGY ON THE DEATH OF
A LATE FAMOUS GENERAL

HIS Grace! impossible! what dead!
Of old age too, and in his bed!
And could that Mighty Warrior fall?
And so inglorious, after all!
5   Well, since he's gone, no matter how,
The last loud trump must wake him now:
And, trust me, as the noise grows stronger,
He'd wish to sleep a little longer.
And could he be indeed so old
10   As by the news-papers we're told?
Threescore, I think, is pretty high;
'Twas time in conscience he should die.
This world he cumber'd long enough;
He burnt his candle to she snuff;
15   And that's the reason, some folks think,
He left behind *so great a s- - - k.*
Behold his funeral appears,
Nor widow's sighs, nor orphan's tears,
Wont at such times each heart to pierce,
20   Attend the progress of his herse.
But what of that, his friends may say,
He had those honours in his day.
True to his profit and his pride,
He made them weep before he dy'd.

25   Come hither, all ye empty things,
Ye bubbles rais'd by breath of Kings;
Who float upon the tide of state,
Come hither, and behold your fate.
Let pride be taught by this rebuke,
30   How very mean a thing's a Duke;
From all his ill-got honours flung,
Turn'd to that dirt from whence he sprung.

Jonathan Swift

THE BEASTS CONFESSION TO THE PRIEST

WHEN Beasts could speak, (the Learned say
They still can do so every Day)
It seems, they had Religion then,
As much as now we find in Men.
5   It happen'd when a Plague broke out,
(Which therefore made them more devout)
The King of Brutes (to make it plain,
Of Quadrupeds I only mean)
By Proclamation gave Command,
10 That ev'ry Subject in the Land
Should to the Priest confess their Sins;
And, thus the pious Wolf begins:
    GOOD Father I must own with Shame,
That, often I have been to blame:
15 I must confess, on *Friday* last,
Wretch that I was, I broke my Fast:
But, I defy the basest Tongue
To prove I did my Neighbour wrong;
Or ever went to seek my Food
20 By Rapine, Theft, or Thirst of Blood.

    THE Ass approaching next, confess'd,
That in his Heart he lov'd a Jest:
A Wag he was, he needs must own,
And could not let a Dunce alone:
25 Sometimes his Friend he would not spare,
And might perhaps be too severe:
But yet, the worst that could be said,
He was a *Wit* both born and bred;
And if it be a Sin or Shame,
30 Nature alone must bear the Blame:
One Fault he hath, is sorry for't,
His Ears are half a Foot too short;
Which could he to the Standard bring,

He'd shew his Face before the K—:
35 Then, for his Voice, there's none disputes
That he's the Nightingal of Brutes.

THE Swine with contrite Heart allow'd,
His Shape and Beauty made him proud:
In Dyet was perhaps too nice,
40 But Gluttony was ne'er his Vice:
In ev'ry Turn of Life content,
And meekly took what Fortune sent:
Inquire through all the Parish round
A better Neighbour ne'er was found:
45 His Vigilance might some displease;
'Tis true, he hated Sloth like Pease.

THE Mimick Ape began his Chatter,
How evil Tongues his Life bespatter:
Much of the cens'ring World complain'd,
50 Who said, his Gravity was feign'd:
Indeed, the Strictness of his Morals
Engag'd him in a hundred Quarrels:
He saw, and he was griev'd to see't,
His Zeal was sometimes indiscreet:
55 He found, his Virtues too severe
For our corrupted Times to bear;
Yet, such a lewd licentious Age
Might well excuse a Stoick's Rage.

THE Goat advanc'd with decent Pace;
60 And, first excus'd his youthful Face;
Forgiveness begg'd, that he appear'd
('Twas Nature's Fault) without a Beard.
'Tis true, he was not much inclin'd
To Fondness for the Female Kind;
65 Not, as his Enemies object,
From Chance, or natural Defect
Not by his frigid Constitution;
But, through a pious Resolution;
For, he had made a holy Vow

70   Of Chastity, as Monks do now;
      Which he resolv'd to keep for ever hence,
      As strictly too; as doth *his Reverence.

      APPLY the Tale, and you shall find
      How just it suits with human Kind.
75   Some Faults we own: But, can you guess?
      Why? —Virtues carry'd to Excess;
      Wherewith our Vanity endows us,
      Though neither Foe nor Friend allows us.

      THE Lawyer swears, you may rely on't,
80   He never squeez'd a needy Clyent:
      And, this he makes his constant Rule;
      For which his Brethren call him Fool:
      His Conscience always was so nice,
      He freely gave the Poor Advice;
85   By which he lost, he may affirm,
      A hundred Fees last *Easter* Term.
      While others of the learned Robe
      Would break the Patience of a *Job,*
      No Pleader at the Bar could match
90   His Diligence and quick Dispatch;
      Ne'er kept a Cause, he well may boast,
      Above a Term or two at most.

      THE cringing Knave who seeks a Place
      Without Success; thus tells his Case:
95   Why should he longer mince the Matter?
      He fail'd, because he could not flatter:
      He had not learn'd to turn his Coat,
      Nor for a Party give his Vote:
      His Crime he quickly understood;
100   Too zealous for the Nation's Good:
      He found, the Ministers resent it,
      Yet could not for his Heart repent it.

* *The Priest his Confessor.*

THE Chaplain vows, he cannot fawn,
Though it would raise him to the Lawn:

105 He pass'd his Hours among his Books;
You find it in his meagre Looks:
He might, if he were worldly-wise,
Preferment get, and spare his Eyes:
But own'd, he had a stubborn Spirit
110 That made him trust alone in Merit:
Would rise by Merit to Promotion;
Alass! a meer Chymerick Notion.

THE Doctor, if you will believe him,
Confess'd a Sin, and God forgive him:
115 Call'd up at Mid-night, ran to save
A blind old Beggar from the Grave:
But, see how *Satan* spreads his Snares;
He quite forgot to say his Pray'rs.
He cannot help it for his Heart
120 Sometimes to act the Parson's Part:
Quotes from the Bible many a Sentence
That moves his Patients to Repentance:
And, when his Med'cines do no good,
Supports their Minds with heav'nly Food.
125 At which, however well intended,
He hears the Clergy are offended;
And grown so bold behind his Back
To call him Hypocrite and Quack.
In his own Church he keeps a Seat;
130 Says Grace before, and after Meat;
And calls, without affecting Airs,
His Houshold twice a Day to Pray'rs.
He shuns Apothecary's Shops;
And hates to cram the Sick with Slops:
135 He scorns to make his Art a Trade;
Nor bribes my Lady's fav'rite Maid.
Old Nurse-keepers would never hire
To recommend him to the Squire;

Which others, whom he will not name,
140 Have often practis'd to their Shame.
  THE Statesman tells you with a *Sneer,*
His Fault is to be too *Sincere;*
And, having no sinister Ends,
Is apt to disoblige his Friends.
145 The Nation's Good, his Master's Glory,
Without Regard to *Whig* or *Tory,*
Were all the Schemes he had in View;
Yet he was seconded by few:
Though some had spread a thousand Lyes;
150 'Twas *He* defeated the EXCISE.
'Twas known, tho' he had born Aspersion;
That, *Standing Troops* were his Aversion:
His Practice was, in ev'ry Station
To serve the King, and please the Nation.
155 Though hard to find in ev'ry Case
The fittest Man to fill a Place:
His Promises he ne'er forgot,
But took Memorials on the Spot:
His Enemies, for want of Charity,
160 Said, he affected Popularity:
'Tis true, the People understood,
That all he did was for their Good;
Their kind Affections he has try'd;
No Love is lost on either Side.
165 He came to Court with Fortune clear,
Which now he runs out every Year;
Must, at the Rate that he goes on,
Inevitably be undone.
Oh! if his Majesty would please
170 To give him but a Writ of Ease,
Would grant him Licence to retire,
As it hath long been his Desire,
By fair Accounts it would be found
He's poorer by ten thousand Pound.
175 He owns, and hopes it is no Sin,

He ne'er was partial to his Kin;
He thought it base for Men in Stations,
To crowd the Court with their Relations:
His Country was his dearest Mother,
180 And ev'ry virtuous Man his Brother:
Through Modesty, or aukward Shame,
(For which he owns himself to blame)
He found the wisest Men he could,
Without Respect to Friends, or Blood,
195 Nor ever acts on private Views,
When he hath Liberty to chuse.

THE Sharper swore he hated Play,
Except to pass an Hour away:
And, well he might; for to his Cost,
190 By want of Skill, he always lost:
He heard, there was a Club of Cheats
Who had contriv'd a thousand Feats;
Could change the Stock, or cog a Dye,
And thus deceive the sharpest Eye:
195 No Wonder how his Fortune sunk,
His Brothers fleece him when he's drunk.

I OWN, the Moral not exact;
Besides, the Tale is false in Fact;
And, so absurd, that could I raise up
200 From Fields *Elyzian,* fabling *Esop;*
I would accuse him to his Face
For libelling the *Four-foot* Race.
Creatures of ev'ry Kind but ours
Well comprehend their nat'ral Powers;
205 While We, whom *Reason* ought to sway,
Mistake our Talents ev'ry Day:
The Ass was never known so stupid
To act the Part of *Tray,* or *Cupid;*
Nor leaps upon his Master's Lap,
210 There to be stroak'd and fed with Pap;
As *Esop* would the World perswade;

He better understands his Trade:
Nor comes whene'er his Lady whistles;
But, carries Loads, and feeds on Thistles;
215 Our Author's Meaning, I presume, is
A Creature *bipes et implumis;
Wherein the Moralist design'd
A Compliment on Human-Kind:
For, here he owns, that now and then
220 **Beasts may *degen'rate* into Men.

* *A Definition of Man, disapproved by all Logicians. Homo est Animal bipes, implume, erecto vultu.*
** *Vide* Gulliver *in his Account of the* Houyhnhnms.

Alexander Pope

FRAGMENT OF A SATIRE

I F meagre *Gildon* draws his venal Quill,
I wish the Man a Dinner, and sit still.
If dreadful *Dennis* raves in furious Fret,
I'll answer *Dennis* when I am in Debt.
5 'Tis Hunger, and not Malice, makes them print,
And who'll wage War with *Bedlam* or the *Mint?*
    Should some more sober Criticks come abroad,
If wrong, I smile; if right, I kiss the Rod.
Pains, Reading, Study, are their just Pretence,
10 And all they want is Spirit, Taste, and Sense.
Commas and *Points* they set exactly right;
And 'twere a Sin to rob them of their *Mite.*
Yet ne'er one Sprig of Laurel grac'd those Ribbalds,
From slashing *B*−*y* down to pidling *Tibbalds:*
15 Who thinks he *reads* when he but *scans* and *spells,*
A Word-catcher, that lives on Syllables.
Yet ev'n this Creature may some Notice claim,
Wrapt round and sanctify'd with *Shakespear*'s Name;

85

Pretty, in Amber to observe the forms
20 Of Hairs, or Straws, or Dirt, or Grubs, or Worms:
The *Thing,* we know, is neither rich nor rare,
But wonder how the Devil it got there.
　　Are others angry? I excuse them too,
Well may they rage; I give them *but* their Due.
25 Each Man's true Merit 'tis not hard to find;
But each Man's secret Standard in his Mind,
That casting Weight, Pride adds to Emptiness;
This, who can *gratify?* For who can *guess?*
The Wretch whom pilfer'd Pastorals renown,
30 Who turns a *Persian* Tale for half a Crown,
Just writes to make his Barrenness appear,
And strains, from hard bound Brains, six Lines a Year;
In Sense still wanting, tho' he lives on Theft,
Steals much, spends little, yet has nothing left:
35 *Johnson,* who now to Sense, now Nonsense leaning,
Means not, but blunders round about a Meaning;
And he, whose Fustian's so sublimely bad,
It is not Poetry, but Prose run mad:
Should modest Satire bid all these *translate,*
40 And own that nine such Poets make a *Tate;*
How would they fume, and stamp, and roar, and chafe!
How would they swear, not *Congreve's* self was safe!
　　Peace to all such! but were there one, whose Fires
Apollo kindled, and fair *Fame* inspires,
45 Blest with each Talent, and each Art to please,
And born to write, converse, and live with ease;
Should such a Man, too fond to rule alone,
Bear, like the *Turk,* no Brother near the Throne;
View him with scornful, yet with fearful eyes,
50 And hate for Arts that caus'd himself to rise;
Damn with faint Praise, assent with civil Leer,
And without sneering, teach the rest to sneer;
Wishing to wound, and yet afraid to strike,
Just hint a Fault, and hesitate Dislike;
55 Alike reserv'd to blame, or to commend,

A tim'rous Foe, and a suspicious Friend,
Dreading ev'n Fools, by Flatterers besieg'd,
And so obliging that he ne'er oblig'd:
Who, if two Wits on rival Themes contest,
60 Approves of each, but likes the worst the best;
Like *Cato* gives his *little Senate* Laws,
And sits attentive to his own Applause;
While Wits and Templars ev'ry Sentence raise,
And wonder with a foolish Face of Praise.
65 What Pity, Heav'n! if such a Man there be.
Who would not weep, if *A—n* were he?

Alexander Pope

THE FIRST SATIRE OF THE SECOND BOOK
OF HORACE IMITATED

P. T H E R E are (I scarce can think it, but am told)
There are to whom my Satire seems too bold,
Scarce to wise *Peter* complaisant enough,
And something said of *Chartres* much too rough.
5 The Lines are weak, another's pleas'd to say,
Lord *Fanny* spins a thousand such a Day.
Tim'rous by Nature, of the Rich in awe,
I come to Council learned in the Law.
You'll give me, like a Friend both sage and free,
10 Advice; and (as you use) without a Fee.
F. I'd write no more.

                    P. Not write? but then I *think*,
And for my Soul I cannot sleep a wink.
I nod in Company, I wake at Night,
Fools rush into my Head, and so I write.

15   *F.* You could not do a worse thing for your Life.
Why, if the Nights seem tedious—take a Wife;
Or rather truly, if your Point be Rest,
Lettuce and Cowslip Wine; *Probatum est.*

But talk with *Celsus, Celsus* will advise
20 Hartshorn, or something that shall close your Eyes.
Or if you needs must write, write C Æ S A R's Praise:
You'll gain at least a *Knighthood,* or the *Bays.*

    P. What? like Sir *Richard,* rumbling, rough and fierce,
With A R M S, and G E O R G E, and B R U N S W I C K crowd the Verse
25 Rend with tremendous Sound your ears asunder,
With Gun, Drum, Trumpet, Blunderbuss & Thunder?
Or nobly wild, with *Budgell's* Fire and Force,
Paint Angels trembling round his *falling Horse?*

    F. Then all your Muse's softer Art display,
30 Let *Carolina* smooth the tuneful Lay,
Lull with *Amelia's* liquid Name the Nine,
And sweetly flow through all the Royal Line.

    P. Alas! few Verses touch their nicer Ear;
They scarce can bear their *Laureate* twice a Year:
35 And justly C Æ S A R scorns the Poet's Lays,
It is to *History* he trusts for Praise.

    F. Better be *Cibber,* I'll maintain it still,
Than ridicule all *Taste,* blaspheme *Quadrille,*
Abuse the City's best good Men in Metre,
40 And laugh at Peers that put their Trust in *Peter.*
Ev'n those you touch not, hate you.
                           P. What should ail 'em?

    F. A hundred smart in *Timon* and in *Balaam:*
The fewer still you name, you wound the more;
Bond is but one, but *Harpax* is a Score.

45   *P.* Each Mortal has his Pleasure: None deny
Scarsdale his Bottle, *Darty* his Ham-Pye;
Ridotta sips and dances, till she see
The doubling Lustres dance as fast as she;
F—loves the *Senate, Hockley-Hole* his Brother
50 Like in all else, as one Egg to another.
I love to pour out all myself, as plain
As downright *Shippen,* or as old *Montagne.*
In them, as certain to be lov'd as seen,
The Soul stood forth, nor kept a Thought within;

55 In me what Spots (for Spots I have) appear,
    Will prove at least the Medium must be clear.
    In this impartial Glass, my Muse intends
    Fair to expose myself, my Foes, my Friends;
    Publish the present Age, but where my Text
60 Is Vice too high, reserve it for the next:
    My Foes shall wish my Life a longer date,
    And ev'ry Friend the less lament my Fate.
        My Head and Heart thus flowing thro' my Quill,
    Verse-man or Prose-man, term me which you will,
65 Papist or Protestant, or both between,
    Like good *Erasmus* in an honest Mean,
    In Moderation placing all my Glory,
    While Tories call me Whig, and Whigs a Tory.
        Satire's my Weapon, but I'm too discreet
70 To run a Muck, and tilt at all I meet;
    I only wear it in a Land of Hectors,
    Thieves, Supercargoes, Sharpers, and Directors.
    Save but our *Army!* and let *Jove* incrust
    Swords, Pikes, and Guns, with everlasting Rust!
75 Peace is my dear Delight—not *Fleury*'s more:
    But touch me, and no Minister so sore.
    Who-e'er offends, at some unlucky Time
    Slides into Verse, and hitches in a Rhyme,
    Sacred to Ridicule! his whole Life long,
80 And the sad Burthen of some merry Song.
        Slander or Poyson, dread from *Delia*'s Rage,
    Hard Words or Hanging, if your Judge be *Page*
    From furious *Sappho* scarce a milder Fate,
    P—x'd by her Love, or libell'd by her Hate:
85 Its proper Pow'r to hurt, each Creature feels,
    Bulls aim their horns, and Asses lift their heels,
    'Tis a Bear's Talent not to kick, but hug,
    And no man wonders he's not stung by Pug:
    So drink with *Waters,* or with *Chartres* eat,
90 They'll never poison you, they'll only cheat.
        Then learned Sir! (to cut the Matter short)

What-e'er my Fate, or well or ill at Court,
Whether old Age, with faint, but chearful Ray,
Attends to gild the Evening of my Day,
95   Or Death's black Wing already be display'd
To wrap me in the Universal Shade;
Whether the darken'd Room to muse invite,
Or whiten'd Wall provoke the Skew'r to write,
In Durance, Exile, Bedlam, or the Mint,
100   Like *Lee* or *Budgell,* I will Rhyme and Print.
      F. Alas young Man! your Days can ne'r be long,
In Flow'r of Age you perish for a Song!
Plums, and Directors, *Shylock* and his Wife,
Will club their Testers, now, to take your Life!
105   *P.* What? arm'd for *Virtue* when I point the Pen,
Brand the bold Front of shameless, guilty Men,
Dash the proud Gamester in his gilded Car,
Bare the mean Heart that lurks beneath a Star;
Can there be wanting to defend Her Cause,
110   Lights of the Church, or Guardians of the Laws?
Could pension'd *Boileau* lash in honest Strain
Flatt'rers and Bigots ev'n in *Louis'* Reign?
Could Laureate *Dryden* Pimp and Fry'r engage,
Yet neither *Charles* nor *James* be in a Rage?
115   And I not strip the Gilding off a Knave,
Un-plac'd, un-pension'd, no Man's Heir, or Slave?
I will, or perish in the gen'rous Cause.
Hear this, and tremble! you, who 'scape the Laws.
Yes, while I live, no rich or noble knave
120   Shall walk the World, in credit, to his grave.
To VIRTUE ONLY and HER FRIENDS, A FRIEND,
The World beside may murmur, or commend.
Know, all the distant Din that World can keep
Rolls o'er my *Grotto,* and but sooths my Sleep.
125   There, my Retreat the best Companions grace,
Chiefs, out of War, and Statesmen, out of Place.
There *St. John* mingles with my friendly Bowl,
The Feast of Reason and the Flow of Soul:

And He, whose Lightning pierc'd th' *Iberian* Lines,
130   Now, forms my Quincunx, and now ranks my Vines,
Or tames the Genius of the stubborn Plain,
Almost as quickly, as he conquer'd *Spain.*
      Envy must own, I live among the Great,
No Pimp of Pleasure, and no Spy of State,
135   With Eyes that pry not, Tongue that ne'er repeats,
Fond to spread Friendships, but to cover Heats,
To help who want, to forward who excel;
This, all who know me, know; who love me, tell;
And who unknown defame me, let them be
140   Scriblers or Peers, alike are *Mob* to me.
This is my Plea, on this I rest my Cause—
What saith my Council learned in the Laws?
      F. Your Plea is good. But still I say, beware!
Laws are explain'd by Men—so have a care.
145   It stands on record, that in *Richard*'s Times
A Man was hang'd for very honest Rhymes.
Consult the Statute: *quart.* I think it is,
Edwardi Sext. or prim. & quint. Eliz:
See *Libels, Satires*—here you have it—read.
150   *P. Libels* and *Satires!* lawless Things indeed!
But grave *Epistles,* bringing Vice to light,
Such as a *King* might read, a *Bishop* write,
Such as Sir *Robert* would approve—
                                    F. Indeed?
The Case is alter'd—you may then proceed.
155   In such a Cause the Plaintiff will be hiss'd,
My Lords the Judges laugh, and you're dismiss'd.

Anonymous.

THE VICAR OF BRAY

IN good King Charles's golden days,
When loyalty no harm meant;

A furious high-church man I was,
  And so I gain'd preferment.
5 Unto my flock I daily preach'd,
  Kings are by God appointed,
And damn'd are those who dare resist,
  Or touch the Lord's anointed.
    And this is law, I will maintain
10   Unto my dying day, Sir,
    That whatsoever King shall reign,
      I will be Vicar of Bray, Sir!

When Royal James possessed the crown,
  And popery grew in fashion;
15 The penal law I houted down,
  And read the declaration:
The Church of Rome, I found would fit,
  Full well my constitution,
And I had been a Jesuit,
20   But for the Revolution.
      And this is law, &c.

When William our deliverer came,
  To heal the nation's grievance,
I turned the cat in pan again,
25   And swore to him allegiance:
Old principles I did revoke,
  Set conscience at a distance,
Passive obedience is a joke,
  A jest is non-resistance.
30   And this is law, &c.

When glorious Ann became our Queen,
  The Church of England's glory,
Another face of things was seen,
  And I became a Tory:
35 Occasional conformists base,
  I damn'd, and moderation,
And thought the church in danger was,

From such prevarication.
    And this is law, &c.

40 When George in pudding time came o'er,
        And moderate men looked big, Sir,
    My principles I chang'd once more,
        And so became a Whig, Sir:
    And thus preferment I procur'd,
45   From our Faith's Great Defender,
    And almost every day abjur'd
        The Pope, and the Pretender.
            And this is law, &c.

    The illustrious House of Hanover,
50   And Protestant succession,
    To these I lustily will swear,
        Whilst they can keep possession:
    For in my faith, and loyalty,
        I never once will falter,
55 But George, my lawful King shall be,
        Except the times should alter.
            And this is law, &c.

Samuel Johnson

LONDON:

A POEM IN IMITATION OF THE THIRD
SATIRE OF JUVENAL

*Quis ineptae
Tam patiens urbis, tam ferreus ut teneat se?*
                    JUVENAL.

Tho' grief and fondness in my breast rebel,
When injur'd Thales bids the town farewell,
Yet still my calmer thoughts his choice commend,
I praise the hermit, but regret the friend,

5   Resolved at length, from vice and London far,
    To breathe in distant fields a purer air,
    And, fix'd on Cambria's solitary shore,
    Give to St. David one true Briton more.
        For who would leave, unbrib'd, Hibernia's land,
10 Or change the rocks of Scotland for the Strand?
    There none are swept by sudden fate away,
    But all whom hunger spares, with age decay:
    Here malice, rapine, accident, conspire,
    And now a rabble rages, now a fire;
15 Their ambush here relentless ruffians lay,
    And here the fell attorney prowls for prey;
    Here falling houses thunder on your head,
    And here a female atheist talks you dead.
        While Thales waits the wherry that contains
20 Of dissipated wealth the small remains,
    On Thames's banks, in silent thought we stood,
    Where Greenwich smiles upon the silver flood:
    Struck with the seat that gave *Eliza birth,
    We kneel, and kiss the consecrated earth;
25 In pleasing dreams the blissful age renew,
    And call Britannia's glories back to view;
    Behold her cross triumphant on the main,
    The guard of commerce, and the dread of Spain,
    Ere masquerades debauch'd, excise oppress'd,
30 Or English honour grew a standing jest.
        A transient calm the happy scenes bestow,
    And for a moment lull the sense of woe.
    At length awaking, with contemptuous frown,
    Indignant Thales eyes the neighb'ring town.
35   Since worth, he cries, in these degen'rate days,
    Wants ev'n the cheap reward of empty praise;
    In those curs'd walls, devote to vice and gain,
    Since unrewarded science toils in vain;
    Since hope but sooths to double my distress,

* Queen Elizabeth born at Greenwich.

40 And ev'ry moment leaves my little less;
    While yet my steddy steps no staff sustains,
    And life still vig'rous revels in my veins;
    Grant me, kind heaven, to find some happier place,
    Where honesty and sense are no disgrace;
45 Some pleasing bank where verdant osiers play,
    Some peaceful vale with nature's paintings gay;
    Where once the harrass'd Briton found repose,
    And safe in poverty defy'd his foes;
    Some secret cell, ye pow'rs, indulgent give.
50 Let———live here, for———has learn'd to live.
    Here let those reign, whom pensions can incite
    To vote a patriot black, a courtier white;
    Explain their country's dear-bought rights away,
    And plead for pirates* in the face of day;
55 With slavish tenets taint our poison'd youth,
    And lend a lye the confidence of truth.
        Let such raise palaces, and manors buy,
    Collect a tax, or farm a lottery,
    With warbling eunuchs fill a licens'd stage,
60 And lull to servitude a thoughtless age.
        Heroes, proceed! what bounds your pride shall hold?
    What check restrain your thirst of pow'r and gold?
    Behold rebellious virtue quite o'erthrown,
    Behold our fame, our wealth, our lives your own.
65   To such, a groaning nation's spoils are giv'n,
    When publick crimes inflame the wrath of heav'n:
    But what, my friend, what hope remains for me,
    Who start at theft, and blush at perjury?
    Who scarce forbear, tho' Britain's Court he sing,
70 To pluck a titled poet's borrow'd wing;
    A statesman's logick unconvinc'd can hear,
    And dare to slumber o'er the Gazetteer;**
    Despise a fool in half his pension dress'd,

---

* The invasions of the Spaniards were defended in the houses of Parliament.
** The paper which at that time contained apologies for the Court.

And strive in vain to laugh at H——y's jest.
75 Others with softer smiles, and subtler art,
Can sap the principles, or taint the heart;
With more address a lover's note convey,
Or bribe a virgin's innocence away.
Well may they rise, while I, whose rustick tongue
80 Ne'er knew to puzzle right, or varnish wrong,
Spurn'd as a begger, dreaded as a spy,
Live unregarded, unlamented die.

For what but social guilt the friend endears?
Who shares Orgilio's crimes, his fortune shares.
85 But thou, should tempting villainy present
All Marlb'rough hoarded, or all Villiers spent,
Turn from the glitt'ring bribe thy scornful eye,
Nor sell for gold, what gold could never buy,
The peaceful slumber, self-approving day,
90 Unsullied fame, and conscience ever gay.

The cheated nation's happy fav'rites, see!
Mark whom the great caress, who frown on me!
London! the needy villain's gen'ral home,
The common shore of Paris and of Rome;
95 With eager thirst, by folly or by fate,
Sucks in the dregs of each corrupted state.
Forgive my transports on a theme like this,
I cannot bear a French metropolis.

Illustrious Edward! from the realms of day,
100 The land of heroes and of saints survey;
Nor hope the British lineaments to trace,
The rustick grandeur, or the surly grace,
But lost in thoughtless ease, and empty show,
Behold the warrior dwindled to a beau;
105 Sense, freedom, piety, refin'd away,
Of France the mimick, and of Spain the prey.

All that at home no more can beg or steal,
Or like a gibbet better than a wheel;
Hiss'd from the stage, or hooted from the court,
110 Their air, their dress, their politicks import;

Obsequious, artful, voluble and gay,
On Britain's fond credulity they prey.
No gainful trade their industry can 'scape,
They sing, they dance, clean shoes, or cure a clap;
115   All sciences a fasting Monsieur knows,
And bid him go to hell, to hell he goes.
     Ah! what avails it, that, from slav'ry far,
I drew the breath of life in English air;
Was early taught a Briton's right to prize,
120   And lisp the tale of Henry's victories;
If the gull'd conqueror receives the chain,
And flattery subdues when arms are vain?
     Studious to please, and ready to submit,
The supple Gaul was born a parasite:
125   Still to his int'rest true, where'er he goes,
Wit, brav'ry, worth, his lavish tongue bestows;
In ev'ry face a thousand graces shine,
From ev'ry tongue flows harmony divine.
These arts in vain our rugged natives try,
130   Strain out with fault'ring diffidence a lye,
And get a kick for aukward flattery.
     Besides, with justice, this discerning age
Admires their wond'rous talents for the stage:
Well may they venture on the mimick's art,
135   Who play from morn to night a borrow'd part;
Practis'd their master's notions to embrace,
Repeat his maxims, and reflect his face;
With ev'ry wild absurdity comply,
And view each object with another's eye;
140   To shake with laughter ere the jest they hear,
To pour at will the counterfeited tear,
And as their patron hints the cold or heat,
To shake in dog-days, in December sweat.
     How, when competitors like these contend,
145   Can surly virtue hope to fix a friend?
Slaves that with serious impudence beguile,
And lye without a blush, without a smile;

Exalt each trifle, ev'ry vice adore,
Your taste in snuff, your judgment in a whore;
150 Can Balbo's eloquence applaud, and swear
He gropes his breeches with a monarch's air.
    For arts like these preferr'd, admir'd, caress'd,
They first invade your table, then your breast;
Explore your secrets with insidious art,
155 Watch the weak hour, and ransack all the heart;
Then soon your ill-plac'd confidence repay,
Commence your lords, and govern or betray.
    By numbers here from shame or censure free,
All crimes are safe, but hated poverty.
160 This, only this, the rigid law pursues,
This, only this, provokes the snarling muse.
The sober trader at a tatter'd cloak,
Wakes from his dream, and labours for a joke;
With brisker air the silken courtiers gaze,
165 And turn the varied taunt a thousand ways.
Of all the griefs that harrass the distress'd,
Sure the most bitter is a scornful jest;
Fate never wounds more deep the gen'rous heart,
Than when a blockhead's insult points the dart.
170   Has heaven reserv'd, in pity to the poor,
No pathless waste, or undiscover'd shore;
No secret island in the boundless main?
No peaceful desart yet unclaim'd by Spain?*
Quick let us rise, the happy seats explore,
175 And bear oppression's insolence no more.
This mournful truth is ev'ry where confess'd,
SLOW RISES WORTH, BY POVERTY DEPRESS'D:
But here more slow, where all are slaves to gold,
Where looks are merchandise, and smiles are sold;
180 Where won by bribes, by flatteries implor'd,
The groom retails the favours of his lord.

* The Spaniards at this time were said to make claim to some of our American provinces.

But hark! th' affrighted crowd's tumultuous cries
Roll thro' the streets, and thunder to the skies;
Rais'd from some pleasing dream of wealth and pow'r,
185 Some pompous palace, or some blissful bow'r,
Aghast you start, and scarce with aking sight
Sustain th' approaching fire's tremendous light;
Swift from pursuing horrors take your way,
And leave your little all to flames a prey;
190 Then thro' the world a wretched vagrant roam,
For where can starving merit find a home?
In vain your mournful narrative disclose,
While all neglect, and most insult your woes.
Should heaven's just bolts Orgilio's wealth confound,
195 And spread his flaming palace on the ground,
Swift o'er the land the dismal rumour flies,
And publick mournings pacify the skies;
The laureat tribe in servile verse relate,
How virtue wars with persecuting fate;
200 With well-feign'd gratitude the pension'd band
Refund the plunder of the begger'd land.
See! while he builds, the gaudy vassals come,
And crowd with sudden wealth the rising dome;
The price of boroughs and of souls restore,
205 And raise his treasures higher than before.
Now bless'd with all the baubles of the great,
The polish'd marble, and the shining plate,
Orgilio sees the golden pile aspire,
And hopes from angry heav'n another fire.
210 Could'st thou resign the park and play content,
For the fair banks of Severn or of Trent;
There might'st thou find some elegant retreat,
Some hireling senator's deserted seat;
And stretch thy prospects o'er the smiling land,
215 For less than rent the dungeons of the Strand;
There prune thy walks, support thy drooping flow'rs,
Direct thy rivulets, and twine thy bow'rs;
And, while thy grounds a cheap repast afford,

Despise the dainties of a venal lord:
220 There ev'ry bush with nature's musick rings,
There ev'ry breeze bears health upon its wings;
On all thy hours security shall smile,
And bless thine evening walk and morning toil.
　　Prepare for death, if here at night you roam,
225 And sign your will before you sup from home.
Some fiery fop, with new commission vain,
Who sleeps on brambles till he kills his man;
Some frolick drunkard, reeling from a feast,
Provokes a broil, and stabs you for a jest.
230 Yet ev'n these heroes, mischievously gay,
Lords of the street, and terrors of the way;
Flush'd as they are with folly, youth and wine,
Their prudent insults to the poor confine;
Afar they mark the flambeau's bright approach,
235 And shun the shining train, and golden coach.
　　In vain, these dangers past, your doors you close,
And hope the balmy blessings of repose:
Cruel with guilt, and daring with despair,
The midnight murd'rer bursts the faithless bar;
240 Invades the sacred hour of silent rest,
And leaves, unseen, a dagger in your breast.
　　Scarce can our fields, such crowds at Tyburn die,
With hemp the gallows and the fleet supply.
Propose your schemes, ye Senatorian band,
245 Whose Ways and Means* support the sinking land;
Lest ropes be wanting in the tempting spring,
To rig another convoy for the k——g.
　　A single jail, in Alfred's golden reign,
Could half the nation's criminals contain;
250 Fair justice then, without constraint ador'd,
Held high the steady scale, but drop'd the sword;
No spies were paid, no special juries known,
Blest age! but ah! how diff'rent from our own!

* A cant term in the House of Commons for methods of raising money.

Much could I add,—but see the boat at hand,
255 The tide retiring, calls me from the land:
Farewell!—When youth, and health, and fortune spent,
Thou fly'st for refuge to the wilds of Kent;
And tir'd like me with follies and with crimes,
In angry numbers warn'st succeeding times;
260 Then shall thy friend, nor thou refuse his aid,
Still foe to vice, forsake his Cambrian shade;
In virtue's cause once more exert his rage,
Thy satire point, and animate thy page.

V. SONGS AND BALLADS

William Congreve

A HUE AND CRY AFTER FAIR AMORET

FAIR *Amoret* is gone astray;
    Pursue and seek her, ev'ry Lover;
I'll tell the Signs by which you may
    The wand'ring Shepherdess discover.

5 Coquet and Coy at once her Air,
    Both study'd, tho' both seem neglected;
Careless she is with artful Care,
    Affecting to seem unaffected.

With Skill her Eyes dart ev'ry Glance,
10   Yet change so soon you'd ne'er suspect 'em
For she'd persuade they wound by Chance,
    Tho' certain Aim and Art direct 'em.

She likes her self, yet others hates
    For that which in herself she prizes;
15 And while she Laughs at them, forgets
    She is the Thing that she despises.

SONG

CRUEL *Amynta,* can you see
    A Heart thus torn which you betray'd?
Love of himself ne'er vanquish'd me,
    But thro' your Eyes the Conquest made.

5 In Ambush there the Traitor lay,
    Where I was led by faithless Smiles:
No Wretches are so lost as they,
    Whom much Security beguiles.

SONG

PIous *Selinda* goes to Pray'rs,
    If I but ask the Favour;
And yet the tender Fool's in Tears,
    When she believes I'll leave her.

5 Wou'd I were free from this Restraint,
    Or else had Hopes to win her;
Wou'd she cou'd make of me a Saint,
    Or I of her a Sinner.

Anne Countess of Winchilsea
A SONG

Miranda hides her from the Sun,
    Beneath those shady beaches nigh,
Whilst I, by her bright rayes undone,
    Can no where for refreshment fly.

5 In that fair grove, att height of noone,
    His fiercest glorys she defies;
I have alas! such shelter none,
    No safe umbrella, 'gainst her eyes.

Thus, does th' unequal hand of fate
10   Refuse itts' favours to devide,
Giving to her a safe retreat,
    And all ofensive arms beside.

Matthew Prior

CUPID MISTAKEN

AS after Noon, one Summer's Day,
    VENUS stood bathing in a River;
CUPID a-shooting went that Way,
    New strung his Bow, new fill'd his Quiver.

5   With Skill He chose his sharpest Dart:
        With all his Might his Bow He drew:
    Swift to His beauteous Parent's Heart
        The too well-guided Arrow flew.

    I faint! I die! the Goddess cry'd:
10   O cruel, could'st Thou find none other,
    To wreck thy Spleen on? Parricide!
        Like NERO, Thou hast slain thy Mother.

    Poor CUPID sobbing scarce could speak;
        Indeed, Mamma, I did not know Ye:
15 Alas! how easie my Mistake?
        I took You for your Likeness, CLOE.

TO PHILLIS

    PHILLIS since we have both been kind,
        And of each other had our fill,
    Tell me, what Pleasure you can find;
        In forcing Nature 'gainst her will.

5   'Tis true, you may with Art and Pain,
        Keep in some Glowings of Desire;
    But still, those Glowings, which remain,
        Are only Ashes of the Fire.

    Then let us free each others Soul,
10   And laugh at the dull constant Fool,
    Who would Love's liberty controul,
        And teach us how to whine by Rule.

    Let us no Impositions set,
        Or clogs upon each others Heart;
15 But as for Pleasure first we met;
        So now for Pleasure let us part.

    We both have spent our Stock of Love,
        So consequently should be free,
    Thirsis expects you in yon Grove,
20   And pretty Chloris stays for me.

'SINCE WE YOUR HUSBAND DAILY SEE'

SINCE we your Husband daily see
    So jealous out of Season;
Phillis, let you and I agree,
    To make him so with reason.

5   I'm vext to think, that ev'ry Night,
    A Sot within thy Arms,
Tasting the most Divine delight,
    Should sully all your Charms.

While fretting I must lye alone,
10   Cursing the Pow'rs Divine;
That undeservedly have thrown
    A Pearl unto a Swine.

Then, Phillis, heal my wounded heart,
    My burning Passion cool;
15   Let me at least in thee have part,
    With thy insipid Fool.

Let him, by night, his Joys pursue,
    And blunder in the dark;
While I, by day, enjoying you,
20   Can see to hit the mark.

[ANSWER TO CLOE JEALOUS]¹

DEAR CLOE, how blubber'd is that pretty Face?
    Thy Cheek all on Fire, and Thy Hair all uncurl'd:
Pr'ythee quit this Caprice; and (as Old FALSTAF says)
    Let Us e'en talk a little like Folks of This World.

5   How can'st Thou presume, Thou hast leave to destroy
    The Beauties, which VENUS but lent to Thy keeping?

1 [The original title is "A Better Answer", referring to the two other poems,
with which this one forms a group ("Cloe Jealous" and "Answer to Cloe
Jealous, in the same Stile. The Author sick.")]

105

Those Looks were design'd to inspire Love and Joy:
    More ord'nary Eyes may serve People for weeping.

     To be vext at a Trifle or two that I writ,
10   Your Judgment at once, and my Passion You wrong:
     You take that for Fact, which will scarce be found Wit:
       Od's Life! must One swear to the Truth of a Song?

     What I speak, my fair CLOE, and what I write, shews
       The Diff'rence there is betwixt Nature and Art:
15   I court others in Verse; but I love Thee in Prose:
       And They have my Whimsies; but Thou hast my Heart.

     The God of us Verse-men (You know Child) the SUN,
       How after his Journeys He sets up his Rest:
     If at Morning o'er Earth 'tis his Fancy to run;
20   At Night he reclines on his THETIS's Breast.

     So when I am weary'd with wand'ring all Day;
       To Thee my Delight in the Evening I come:
     No Matter what Beauties I saw in my Way:
       They were but my Visits; but Thou art my Home.

25   Then finish, Dear CLOE, this Pastoral War;
       And let us like HORACE and LYDIA agree:
     For Thou art a Girl as much brighter than Her,
       As He was a Poet sublimer than Me.

Thomas Parnell

SONG

     WHEN thy Beauty appears
      In its Graces and Airs,
    All bright as an Angel new dropt from the Sky;
     At distance I gaze, and am aw'd by my Fears,
5   So strangely you dazzle my Eye!

But when without Art,
Your kind Thoughts you impart,
When your Love runs in Blushes thro' ev'ry Vein;
When it darts from your Eyes, when it pants in your Heart,
10   Then I know you're a Woman again.

There's a Passion and Pride
In our Sex, (she reply'd,)
And thus (might I gratify both) I wou'd do:
Still an Angel appear to each Lover beside,
15   But still be a Woman to you.

John Gay

A BALLAD[1]

'TWAS when the seas were roaring
  With hollow blasts of wind;
A damsel lay deploring,
  All on a rock reclin'd.
5 Wide o'er the rolling billows
  She cast a wistful look;
Her head was crown'd with willows
  That tremble o'er the brook.

Twelve months are gone and over,
10   And nine long tedious days.
Why didst thou, vent'rous lover,
  Why didst thou trust the seas?
Cease, cease, thou cruel ocean,
  And let my lover rest:
15 Ah! what 's thy troubled motion
  To that within my breast?

The merchant, rob'd of pleasure,
  Sees tempests in despair;

1 [Originally part of the "tragi-comi-pastoral farce" *The What D'Ye Call It.*]

107

But what's the loss of treasure
20   To losing of my dear?
Should you some coast be laid on
        Where gold and di'monds grow,
You'd find a richer maiden,
        But none that loves you so.
25 How can they say that nature
        Has nothing made in vain;
Why then beneath the water
        Should hideous rocks remain?
No eyes the rocks discover,
30   That lurk beneath the deep,
To wreck the wand' ring lover.
        And leave the maid to weep.

All melancholy lying.
        Thus wail'd she for her dear;
35 Repay'd each blast with sighing,
        Each billow with a tear;
When, o'er the white wave stooping,
        His floating corpse she spy'd;
Then like a lily drooping,
40   She bow'd her head, and dy'd.

SWEET WILLIAM'S FAREWELL TO BLACK-EY'D SUSAN

A Ballad

ALL in the *Downs* the fleet was moor'd,
        The streamers waving in the wind,
When black-ey'd *Susan* came aboard.
        Oh! where shall I my true love find!
5 Tell me, ye jovial sailors, tell me true,
If my sweet *William* sails among the crew.

William, who high upon the yard,
        Rock'd with the billow to and fro,
Soon as her well-known voice he heard,

10   He sigh'd and cast his eyes below:
    The cord slides swiftly through his glowing hands,
    And, (quick as lightning,) on the deck he stands.

        So the sweet lark, high-pois'd in air,
            Shuts close his pinions to his breast,
15   (If, chance, his mate's shrill call he hear)
            And drops at once into her nest.
    The noblest Captain in the *British* fleet,
    Might envy *William*'s lip those kisses sweet.

        O *Susan, Susan,* lovely dear,
20   My vows shall ever true remain;
        Let me kiss off that falling tear,
            We only part to meet again.
    Change, as ye list, ye winds; my heart shall be
    The faithful compass that still points to thee.

25   Believe not what the landmen say,
            Who tempt with doubts thy constant mind:
        They'll tell thee, sailors, when away,
            In ev'ry port a mistress find.
    Yes, yes, believe them when they tell thee so,
30 For thou art present wheresoe'er I go.

        If to far *India*'s coast we sail,
            Thy eyes are seen in di'monds bright,
        Thy breath is *Africk*'s spicy gale,
            Thy skin is ivory, so white.
35 Thus ev'ry beauteous object that I view,
    Wakes in my soul some charm of lovely *Sue.*

        Though battel call me from thy arms,
            Let not my pretty *Susan* mourn;
        Though cannons roar, yet safe from harms,
40   *William* shall to his Dear return.
    Love turns aside the balls that round me fly,
    Lest precious tears should drop from *Susan*'s eye.
        The boatswain gave the dreadful word,
            The sails their swelling bosom spread,

45   No longer must she stay aboard:
         They kiss'd, she sigh'd, he hung his head;
Her less'ning boat, unwilling rows to land:
Adieu, she cries! and wav'd her lilly hand.

NEWGATE'S GARLAND[1]

YE Gallants of *Newgate,* whose Fingers are nice,
In diving in Pockets, or cogging of Dice.
Ye Sharpers so rich, who can buy off the Noose,
Ye honester poor Rogues, who die in your Shoes,
5   Attend and draw near,
     Good News ye shall hear,
     How *Jonathan*'s Throat was cut from Ear to Ear;
How *Blueskin*'s sharp Penknife hath set you at Ease,
And every Man round me may rob, if he please.

10   When to the *Old-Bailey* this *Blueskin* was led,
He held up his Hand, his Indictment was read,
Loud rattled his Chains, near him *Jonathan* stood,
For full Forty Pounds was the Price of his Blood.
     Then hopeless of Life,
15   He drew his Penknife,
     And made a sad Widow of *Jonathan*'s Wife.
But Forty Pounds paid her, her Grief shall appease,
And every Man round me may rob, if he please.

Some say there are Courtiers of highest Renown,
20   Who steal the King's Gold, and leave him but a *Crown;*
Some say there are Peers, and some Parliament Men,
Who meet once a Year to rob Courtiers agen:
     Let them all take their Swing,

1 [In the edition reprinted here, the full title runs: "Newgate's Garland: Being a new Ballad. Shewing how Mr. *Jonathan Wild*'s Throat was cut from Ear to Ear with a Penknife, by Mr. *Blake,* alias *Blueskin,* the bold Highwayman, as he stood his Tryal in the *Old-Bailey.*"
Stanzas VI and VII are, very probably, not Gay's but Swift's.]

To pillage the King,
25 And get a Blue Ribbon instead of a String.
Now *Blueskin's* sharp Penknife hath set you at Ease,
And every Man round me may rob, if he please.

Knaves of old, to hide Guilt by their cunning Inventions,
Call'd Briberies Grants, and plain Robberies Pensions;
30 Physicians and Lawyers (who take their Degrees
To be Learned Rogues) call'd their Pilfering, Fees;
    Since this happy Day,
    Now ev'ry Man may
    Rob (as safe as in Office) upon the Highway.
35 For *Blueskin's* sharp Penknife hath set you at Ease,
And every Man round me may rob, if he please.

Some cheat in the Customs, some rob the Excise,
But he who robs both is esteemed most wise.
Church-Wardens, too prudent to hazard the Halter,
40 As yet only venture to steal from the Altar:
    But now to get Gold,
    They may be more bold,
    And rob on the Highway, since *Jonathan's* cold.
For *Blueskin's* sharp Penknife hath set you at Ease,
45 And every man round me may rob, if he please.

Some by publick Revenues, which pass'd through their Hands,
Have purchas'd clean Houses, and bought dirty Lands,
Some to steal from a Charity think it no Sin,
Which, at Home (says the Proverb) does always begin;
50 But, if ever you be
    Assign'd a Trustee,
    Treat not Orphans like Masters of the Chancery.
But take the Highway, and more honestly seise,
For every Man round me may rob, if he please.

55 What a Pother has here been with *Wood* and his Brass,
Who would modestly make a few Half-pennies pass!
The Patent is good, and the Precedent's old.
For *Diomede* changed his Copper for Gold:

But if *Ireland* despise
60   Thy new Half-pennies,
     With more Safety to rob on the Road I advise.
For *Blueskin's* sharp Penknife hath set thee at Ease,
And every Man round me may rob, if he please.

Thomas Tickell

COLIN AND LUCY

Of Leinster, fam'd for maidens fair,
    Bright Lucy was the grace;
Nor e'er did Liffy's limpid stream
    Reflect so sweet a face:
5   Till luckless love, and pining care,
    Impair'd her rosy hue,
Her coral lips, and damask cheeks,
    And eyes of glossy blue.

Oh! have you seen a lilly pale,
10   When beating rains descend?
So droop'd the slow-consuming maid,
    Her life now near its end.
By Lucy warn'd, of flatt'ring swains
    Take heed, ye easy fair:
15   Of vengeance due to broken vows,
    Ye perjur'd swains, beware.

Three times, all in the dead of night,
    A bell was heard to ring;
And shrieking at her window thrice,
20   The raven flap'd his wing.
Too well the love-lorn maiden knew
    The solemn boding sound;
And thus, in dying words, bespoke
    The virgins weeping round:

25   "I hear a voice, you cannot hear,
      Which says, I must not stay;
  I see a hand, you cannot see,
      Which beckons me away.
  By a false heart, and broken vows,
30   In early youth I die:
  Was I to blame, because his bride
      Was thrice as rich as I?

  "Ah, Colin! give not her thy vows,
      Vows due to me alone;
35   Nor thou, fond maid, receive his kiss,
      Nor think him all thy own.
  To-morrow, in the churcn to wed,
      Impatient, both prepare;
  But know, fond maid, and know, false man,
40   That Lucy will be there!

  "Then bear my corse, my comrades, bear,
      This bridegroom blythe to meet,
  He in his wedding-trim so gay,
      I in my winding-sheet."
45   She spoke; she dy'd; her corse was born,
      The bridegroom blythe to meet,
  He in his wedding-trim so gay,
      She in her winding-sheet.

  Then what were perjur'd Colin's thoughts?
50   How were these nuptials kept?
  The bridesmen flock'd round Lucy dead,
      And all the village wept.
  Confusion, shame, remorse, despair,
      At once his bosom swell:
55   The damps of death bedew'd his brow,
      He shook, he groan'd, he fell.

  From the vain bride, (ah bride no more!)
      The varying crimson fled,
  When, stretch'd before her rival's corse,

60   She saw her husband dead.
     Then to his Lucy's new-made grave
        Convey'd by trembling swains,
     One mould with her, beneath one sod,
        For ever he remains.

65   Oft at this grave, the constant hind,
        And plighted maid are seen;
     With garlands gay, and true-love knots,
        They deck the sacred green;
     But, swain forsworn, whoe'er thou art,
70   This hallow'd spot forbear;
     Remember Colin's dreadful fate,
        And fear to meet him there.

Henry Carey

THE BALLAD OF SALLY IN OUR ALLEY

Of all the Girls that are so smart
     There's none like pretty Sally,
She is the Darling of my Heart,
     And she lives in our Alley.
5   There is no Lady in the Land,
     Is half so sweet as Sally,
She is the Darling of my Heart,
     And she lives in our Alley.

Her Father he makes Cabbage-nets,
10   And through the Streets does cry 'em;
Her Mother she sells Laces long,
     To such as please to buy 'em:
But sure such Folks could ne'er beget
     So sweet a Girl as Sally!
15   She is the Darling of my Heart,
     And she lives in our Alley.

When she is by I leave my Work,
　　(I love her so sincerely)
My Master comes like any Turk,
20　　And bangs me most severely;
But, let him bang his Belly-full,
　　I'll bear it all for Sally;
She is the Darling of my Heart,
　　And she lives in our Alley.

25　Of all the Days that's in the Week,
　　I dearly love but one Day,
And that's the Day that comes betwixt
　　A Saturday and Monday;
For then I'm dress'd, all in my best,
30　　To walk abroad with Sally;
She is the Darling of my Heart,
　　And she lives in our Alley.

My Master carries me to Church,
　　And often am I blamed,
35　Because I leave him in the lurch,
　　As soon as Text is named:
I leave the Church in Sermon time,
　　And slink away to Sally;
She is the Darling of my Heart.
40　　And she lives in our Alley.

When Christmas comes about again,
　　O then I shall have Money;
I'll hoard it up, and box and all
　　I'll give it to my Honey:
45　And, would it were ten thousand Pounds,
　　I'd give it all to Sally;
She is the Darling of my Heart,
　　And she lives in our Alley.

My Master and the Neighbours all
50　　Make game of me and Sally;
And (but for her) I'd better be

A Slave and row a Galley:
But when my seven long Years are out,
O then I'll marry Sally!
55   O then we'll wed and then we'll bed,
But not in our Alley.

Anonymous.

A NEW SONG ENTITLED THE WARMING PAN

When *Jemmy* the Second, not *Jemmy* the First,
With Vexations and Poxes, and Impotence Curs'd,
Saw the good Cause must end, which so well he began,
Swore the Church, since he cou'd not, should get him a son
5   *Derry down, down* etc.

To work went the Church on her Majesty's Womb,
By her true Representations, Fryers from *Rome;*
But [though] they well warm'd, her true Catholic Mettle,
They never could make the Meat boil in the Kettle.
10   *Derry Down*

But since it was determin'd an Heir must be got,
No matter from *Kettle,* from *Pan,* or from *Pot;*
In Mettles Fertile, the old *JESUITS* clan,
Produc'd a brave Boy, from a *Brass-Warming-Pan*
15   *Derry Down*

But *Old England,* quite harrass'd with Papists before,
The *Brat* being Spurious, would sure bear no more;
But with little *Will's* help, kick'd the spawn of a *Fryer,*
From out of the *Warming Pan* into the Fire.
25   *Derry Down*

Full many a Year, has that *Bastard* been Nurs'd,
By *Paris* and *Rome,* who engender'd him first;
And now they have sent to promote their old Plan,
The Son of the Son, of the *Brass-Warming-Pan*
30   *Derry Down*

116

Oh! *Britains,* reflect, why you drove out the *One!*
And dread the same evils or worse in the *Son;*
Quick, to *Paris,* or *Rome* make your *Perkin* retire,
Or we're out of the *Warming-Pan,* into the *Fire.*
35   *Derry Down*

Sure *Scotland* remembers, the direful Fate,
When they succour'd the *Warming-Pan's* Father of late;
How many to *Tower,* and *Newgate,* were sent,
Some Heads were cut off, and too late did Repent.
40   *Derry Down*

May all be serv'd so, that takes up the Cause,
For *Rome* or the D–l, make daily applause;
Let's firmly unite in the Protestant Case,
Drive *Pretender* to the D–l, keep K. *George* in his place.
45   *Derry Down*

Matthew Prior

JINNY THE JUST

RELEAS'D from the Noise of the Butcher and Baker,
Who, my old friends be thanked, did seldom forsake Her
And from the soft Duns of my Landlord the Quaker

From chiding the footmen and watching the lasses,
5   From Nel that burn't milk too, and Tom that brake glasses
(Sad mischeifs thrô which a good housekeeper passes!)

From some real Care but more fancied vexation
From a life party-colour'd half reason half passion
Here lyes after all the best Wench in the Nation.

10   From the Rhine to the Po, from the Thames to the Rhone
Joanna or Janneton, Jinny or Joan
Twas all one to Her by what name She was known

For the Idiom of words very little She heeded
Provided the Matter She drove at Succeeded,
15   She took and gave languages just as she needed:

So for Kitching and markett for bargain and Sale
She paid English or Dutch or French down on the Nail
But in telling a Story She Sometimes did fail

Then begging excuse as she happen'd to stammer
20   With respect to her betters but none to her Grammer
Her blush helpt Her out and her jargon became Her.

Her habit and mein she Endeavour'd to frame
To the different Gout of the place where she came,
Her outside still chang'd, but her Inside the Same:

25 At the Hague in her Slippers and hair as the mode is
   At Paris all falbalow'd fine as a Goddess
   And at censuring London in Smock sleeves and Bodice

   She order'd affairs that few people could tell
   In what part about Her that mixture did dwell
30 Of Vrough or Mistresse, or Mademoiselle.

   For Her Sirname and race let the Heraults e'n answer,
   Her own proper worth was enough to advance Her,
   And He who lik'd Her little valu'd her Grandsire

   But from what House soever her lineage may come
35 I wish my own Jinny but out of her tomb,
   Thô all her relations were there in her Room.

   Of such terrible beauty She never could boast
   As with absolute sway oer all hearts rules the roast
   When J——bawls out to the Chair for a toast.

40 But of good household features her Person was made
   Nor by faction cry'd up nor of censure afraid
   And her beauty was rather for use than Parade

   Her blood so well mixt and flesh so well pasted
   That tho her Youth faded her comliness lasted
45 The blue was worn off but the plum was well tasted.

   Less smooth then her Skin and Less White then her breast
   Was this polisht stone beneath which she lyes prest
   Stop, reader and sigh while thou think'st on the rest.

   With a just trim of virtue her Soul was endued
50 Not affectedly pious nor Secretly Lewd
   She cutt even between the Coquette, and the Prude

   And Her will with her duty so equally stood
   That Seldom oppos'd she was commonly good
   And did pretty well, doing just what She wou'd.

55 Declining all power She found means to persuade
   Was then most regarded, when most she obey'd,
   The Mistresse in truth when She seem'd but the Maid

119

Such care of her own proper actions she took
That on other folks lives She had no time to look
60 So Censure and Praise were struck out of her book

Her thought still confin'd to it's own little sphere
She minded not who did excell or did err
But just as the Matter related to Her

Then too when her private tribunal was rear'd
65 Her mercy so mixt with her judgement appear'd
That her foes were condemnd and her friend's always clear'd.

Her religion so well with her learning did suit
That in practice sincere, and in controverse mute
She show'd She knew better to live then dispute.

70 Some parts of the Bible by heart she recited
And much in historical Chapters delighted
But in points about faith she was something short sighted

So Notions and modes she referr'd to the Scholes
And in matters of Conscience adher'd to two rules
75 To advise with no biggots and jeast with no fools

And Scrupling but little, enough She beleiv'd;
By Charity ample small sins she retriev'd
And when She had New Cloaths she always receiv'd

Thus still whilst her Morning unseen fled away
80 In ordering the Linnin and making the Tea
That She Scarce could have time for the Psalms of the Day
And while after Dinner the Night came so soon
That half she propos'd very seldom was done
With twenty God bless Me's how this day is gon

85 While she read and accounted and pay'd and abated
Eat and drank, play'd and work't, laught and cry'd, lov'd and hat
As answer'd the End of her being created

In the midst of her Age came a cruell desease
Which neither her broths nor recepts could appease
90 So down dropt her Clay, may her Soul be at Peace

Retire from this Sepulchre all the prophane
Ye that love for debauch or that marry for gain
Retire least Ye trouble the Manes of J——.

But Thou that know'st love above Interest or lust
95 Strew the Myrtle and rose on this once belov'd dust
And shed one pious tear upon Jinny the Just

Tread Soft on her grave, and do right to her honour
Lett neither rude hand nor Ill tongue light upon her
Do all the Small favours that now can be don her

100 And when what Thou lik't Shall return to her Clay
For so Im persuaded She must do one day
What ever fantastic J[ohn] Asgil may Say
When as I have don now thou shalt sett up a Stone
For Something however distinguisht or known
105 May Some pious friend the misfortune bemoan
And make thy Concern by reflexion his own.

Alexander Pope

EPITAPH ON CHARLES EARL OF DORSET

DORSET, the Grace of Courts, the Muses Pride,
Patron of Arts, and Judge of Nature, dy'd!
The Scourge of Pride, tho' sanctify'd or great,
Of Fops in Learning, and of Knaves in State:
5 Yet soft his Nature, tho' severe his Lay,
His Anger moral, and his Wisdom gay.
Blest Satyrist! who touch'd the Mean so true,
As show'd, Vice had his Hate and Pity too.
Blest Courtier! who could King and Country please,
10 Yet sacred keep his Friendships, and his Ease.
Blest Peer! his great Forefathers ev'ry Grace
Reflecting, and reflected in his Race;
Where other Buckhursts, other Dorsets shine,
And Patriots still, or Poets, deck the Line.

EPITAPH ON SIR WILLIAM TRUMBULL

A PLEASING form, a firm, yet cautious mind,
Sincere, tho' prudent, constant, yet resign'd;
Honour unchang'd, a principle profest,
Fix'd to one side, but mod'rate to the rest;
5   An honest Courtier, yet a Patriot too,
Just to his Prince, yet to his Country true;
Fill'd with the sense of age, the fire of youth;
A scorn of wrangling, yet a zeal for truth;
A gen'rous faith, from superstition free,
10 A love to peace, and hate of tyranny;
Such this man was; who now, from earth remov'd,
At length enjoys that liberty he lov'd.

Richard Savage

EPITAPH ON A YOUNG LADY

CLOS'D are those eyes, that beam'd seraphic fire;
Cold is that breast, which gave the world desire;
Mute is the voice, where winning softness warm'd,
Where music melted, and where wisdom charm'd,
5   And lively wit, which, decently confin'd,
No prude e'er thought impure, no friend unkind.
   Cou'd modest knowledge, fair untrifling youth,
Persuasive reason and endearing truth,
Cou'd honour, shewn in friendships most refin'd,
10 And sense, that shields th'attempted virtuous mind,
The social temper never known to strife,
The height'ning graces that embellish life;
Cou'd these have e'er the darts of death defied,
Never, ah! never had *Melinda* died;
15 Nor can she die—ev'n now survives her name,
Immortaliz'd by friendship, love and fame.

James Thomson

TO THE MEMORY OF SIR ISAAC NEWTON

SHALL the great soul of Newton quit this earth
To mingle with his stars, and every Muse,
Astonished into silence, shun the weight
Of honours due to his illustrious name?
5   But what can man? Even now the sons of light,
I strains high warbled to seraphic lyre,
Hail his arrival on the coast of bliss.
Yet am not I deterred, though high the theme,
And sung to harps of angels, for with you,
10 Ethereal flames! ambitious, I aspire
In Nature's general symphony to join.
     And what new wonders can ye show your guest!
Who, while on this dim spot where mortals toil
Clouded in dust, from motion's simple laws
15 Could trace the secret hand of Providence,
Wide-working through this universal frame.
     Have ye not listened while he bound the suns
And planets to their spheres! the unequal task
Of humankind till then. Oft had they rolled
20 O'er erring man the year, and oft disgraced
The pride of schools, before their course was known
Full in its causes and effects to him,
All-piercing sage! who sat not down and dreamed
Romantic schemes, defended by the din
25 Of specious words, and tyranny of names;
But, bidding his amazing mind attend,
And with heroic patience years on years
Deep-searching, saw at last the system dawn,
And shine, of all his race, on him alone.
30   What were his raptures then! how pure! how strong!
And what the triumphs of old Greece and Rome.
By his diminished, but the pride of boys
In some small fray victorious! when instead
Of shattered parcels of this earth usurped

35 By violence unmanly, and sore deeds
    Of cruelty and blood, Nature herself
    Stood all subdued by him, and open laid
    Her every latent glory to his view.
        All intellectual eye, our solar round
40 First gazing through, he, by the blended power
    Of gravitation and projection, saw
    The whole in silent harmony revolve.
    From unassisted vision hid, the moons
    To cheer remoter planets numerous formed,
45 By him in all their mingled tracts were seen.
    He also fixed our wandering Queen of Night,
    Whether she wanes into a scanty orb,
    Or, waxing broad, with her pale shadowy light,
    In a soft deluge overflows the sky.
50 Her every motion clear-discerning, he
    Adjusted to the mutual main and taught
    Why now the mighty mass of waters swells
    Resistless, heaving on the broken rocks,
    And the full river turning—till again
55 The tide revertive, unattracted, leaves
    A yellow waste of idle sands behind.
        Then, breaking hence, he took his ardent flight
    Through the blue infinite; and every star,
    Which the clear concave of a winter's night
60 Pours on the eye, or astronomic tube,
    Far stretching, snatches from the dark abyss,
    Or such as further in successive skies
    To fancy shine alone, at his approach
    Blazed into suns, the living centre each
65 Of an harmonious system—all combined,
    And ruled unerring by that single power
    Which draws the stone projected to the ground.
        O unprofuse magnificence divine!
    O wisdom truly perfect! thus to call
70 From a few causes such a scheme of things,
    Effects so various, beautiful, and great,

An universe complete! And O beloved
Of Heaven! whose well purged penetrating eye
The mystic veil transpiercing, inly scanned
75 The rising, moving, wide-established frame.
    He, first of men, with awful wing pursued
The comet through the long elliptic curve,
As round innumerous worlds he wound his way,
Till, to the forehead of our evening sky
80 Returned, the blazing wonder glares anew,
And o'er the trembling nations shakes dismay.
    The heavens are all his own, from the wide rule
Of whirling vortices and circling spheres
To their first great simplicity restored.
85 The schools astonished stood; but found it vain
To combat still with demonstration strong,
And, unawakened, dream beneath the blaze
Of truth. At once their pleasing visions fled,
With the gay shadows of the morning mixed,
90 When Newton rose, our philosophic sun!
    The aerial flow of sound was known to him,
From whence it first in wavy circles breaks,
Till the touched organ takes the message in.
Nor could the darting beam of speed immense
95 Escape his swift pursuit and measuring eye.
Even Light itself, which every thing displays,
Shone undiscovered, till his brighter mind
Untwisted all the shining robe of day;
And, from the whitening undistinguished blaze,
100 Collecting every ray into his kind,
To the charmed eye educed the gorgeous train
Of parent colours. First the flaming red
Sprung vivid forth; the tawny orange next;
And next delicious yellow; by whose side
105 Fell the kind beams of all-refreshing green.
Then the pure blue, that swells autumnal skies,
Ethereal played; and then, of sadder hue,
Emerged the deepened indigo, as when

The heavy-skirted evening droops with frost;
110 While the last gleamings of refracted light
Died in the fainting violet away.
These, when the clouds distil the rosy shower,
Shine out distinct adown the watery bow;
While o'er our heads the dewy vision bends
115 Delightful, melting on the fields beneath.
Myriads of mingling dyes from these result,
And myriads still remain—infinite source
Of beauty, ever flushing, ever new.
        Did ever poet image aught so fair,
120 Dreaming in whispering groves by the hoarse brook?
Or prophet, to whose rapture heaven descends?
Even now the setting sun and shifting clouds,
Seen, Greenwich, from thy lovely heights; declare
How just, how beauteous the refractive law.
125   The noiseless tide of time, all bearing down
To vast eternity's unbounded sea,
Where the green islands of the happy shine,
He stemmed alone; and, to the source (involved
Deep in primeval gloom) ascending, raised
130 His lights at equal distances, to guide
Historian wildered on his darksome way.
        But who can number up his labours? who
His high discoveries sing? When but a few
Of the deep-studying race can stretch their minds
135 To what he knew—in fancy's lighter thought
How shall the muse then grasp the mighty theme?
        What wonder thence that his devotion swelled
Responsive to his knowledge? For could he
Whose piercing mental eye diffusive saw
140 The finished university of things
In all its order, magnitude, and parts
Forbear incessant to adore that Power
Who fills, sustains, and actuates the whole?
        Say, ye who best can tell, ye happy few,
145 Who saw him in the softest lights of life,

All unwithheld, indulging to his friends
The vast unborrowed treasures of his mind,
Oh, speak the wondrous man! how mild, how calm,
How greatly humble, how divinely good,
150 How firmly stablished on eternal truth;
Fervent in doing well, with every nerve
Still pressing on, forgetful of the past,
And panting for perfection; far above
Those little cares and visionary joys
155 That so perplex the fond impassioned heart
Of ever cheated, ever trusting man.
This, Conduitt, from thy rural hours we hope,
As through the pleasing shade where nature pours
Her every sweet in studious ease you walk,
160 The social passions smiling at thy heart
That glows with all the recollected sage.
    And you, ye hopeless gloomy-minded tribe,
You who, unconscious of those nobler flights
That reach impatient at immortal life,
165 Against the prime endearing privilege
Of being dare contend,—say, can a soul
Of such extensive, deep, tremendous powers,
Enlarging still, be but a finer breath
Of spirits dancing through their tubes awhile,
170 And then for ever lost in vacant air?
    But hark! methinks I hear a warning voice,
Solemn as when some awful change is come,
Sound through the world—' 'Tis done!—the measure's full;
And I resign my charge.'—Ye mouldering stones
175 That build the towering pyramid, the proud
Triumphal arch, the monument effaced
By ruthless ruin, and whate'er supports
The worshipped name of hoar antiquity—
Down to the dust! What grandeur can ye boast
180 While Newton lifts his column to the skies,
Beyond the waste of time. Let no weak drop
Be shed for him. The virgin in her bloom

Cut off, the joyous youth, and darling child—
These are the tombs that claim the tender tear
185 And elegiac song. But Newton calls
For other notes of gratulation high,
That now he wanders through those endless worlds
He here so well descried, and wondering talks,
And hymns their Author with his glad compeers.
190 O Britain's boast! whether with angels thou
Sittest in dread discourse, or fellow-blessed,
Who joy to see the honour of their kind;
Or whether, mounted on cherubic wing,
Thy swift career is with the whirling orbs,
195 Comparing things with things, in rapture lost,
And grateful adoration for that light
So plenteous rayed into thy mind below
From Light Himself; oh, look with pity down
On humankind, a frail erroneous race!
200 Exalt the spirit of a downward world!
O'er thy dejected country chief preside,

And be her Genius called! her studies raise,
Correct her manners, and inspire her youth;
For, though depraved and sunk, she brought thee forth,
205 And glories in thy name! she points thee out
To all her sons, and bids them eye thy star:
While, in expectance of the second life
When time shall be no more, thy sacred dust
Sleeps with her kings, and dignifies the scene.

VII. HYMNS

Joseph Addison

AN ODE

The Spacious Firmament on high,
With all the blue Etherial Sky,
And spangled Heav'ns, a Shining Frame,
Their great Original proclaim:
5 Th'unwearied Sun, from day to day,
Does his Creator's Pow'r display,
And publishes to every Land
The Work of an Almighty Hand.

Soon as the Evening Shades prevail,
10 The Moon takes up the wondrous Tale,
And nightly to the listning Earth
Repeats the Story of her Birth:
Whilst all the Stars that round her burn,
And all the Planets, in their turn,
15 Confirm the Tidings as they rowl,
And spread the Truth from Pole to Pole.

What though, in solemn Silence, all
Move round the dark terrestrial Ball?
What tho' nor real Voice nor Sound
20 Amid their radiant Orbs be found?
In Reason's Ear they all rejoice,
And utter forth a glorious Voice,
For ever singing, as they shine,
'The Hand that made us is Divine'.

Isaac Watts

HYMN

HOW vain are all things here below.
    How false, and yet how fair!
Each Pleasure hath its Poison too,
    And every Sweet a Snare.

5   The brightest Things below the Sky
    Give but a flattering Light;
We should suspect some Danger nigh
    Where we possess Delight.

Our dearest Joys, and nearest Friends,
10   The Partners of our Blood,
How they divide our wavering Minds,
    And leave but half for God.

The Fondness of a Creatures Love,
    How strong it strikes the Sense!
15   Thither the warm Affections move,
    Nor can we call 'em thence.

Dear Saviour, let thy Beauties be
    My Souls Eternal Food;
And Grace command my Heart away
20   From all created Good.

Isaac Watts

A CRADLE HYMN

HUSH! my dear, lie still and slumber,
    Holy angels guard thy bed!
Heavenly blessings without number
    Gently falling on thy head.

5   Sleep, my babe; thy food and raiment,
    House and home, thy friends provide;

All without thy care or payment:
    All thy wants are well supplied.

How much better thou'rt attended
10   Than the Son of God could be,
When from heaven He descended
    And became a child like thee!

Soft and easy is thy cradle:
    Coarse and hard thy Saviour lay,
15 When His birthplace was a stable
    And His softest bed was hay.

Blessèd babe! what glorious features—
    Spotless fair, divinely bright!
Must He dwell with brutal creatures?
20 How could angels bear the sight?

Was there nothing but a manger
    Cursèd sinners could afford
To receive the heavenly stranger?
    Did they thus affront their Lord?

25 Soft, my child: I did not chide thee,
    Though my song might sound too hard;
'Tis thy mother sits beside thee,
    And her arms shall be thy guard.

Yet to read the shameful story
30 How the Jews abused their King,
How they served the Lord of Glory,
    Makes me angry while I sing.

See the kinder shepherds round Him,
    Telling wonders from the sky!
35 Where they sought Him, there they found Him,
    With His Virgin mother by.

See the lovely babe a-dressing;
    Lovely infant, how He smiled!
When He wept, the mother's blessing
40 Soothed and hush'd the holy child.

Lo, He slumbers in His manger,
     Where the hornèd oxen fed:
Peace, my darling; here 's no danger,
     Here 's no ox anear thy bed.

45 'Twas to save thee, child, from dying,
          Save my dear from burning flame,
     Bitter groans and endless crying,
          That thy blest Redeemer came.

     May'st thou live to know and fear Him,
50   Trust and love Him all thy days;
     Then go dwell for ever near Him,
          See His face, and sing His praise!

Henry Needler

A VERNAL HYMN, IN PRAISE OF THE CREATOR

ARISE, my Muse: Awake thy Sleeping Lyre,
And fan with tuneful Airs thy languid Fire.
On daring Pinions rais'd, low Themes despise;
But stretch thy Wings in yon' bright azure Skies.
5 Let not this chearful Prime, these Genial Days,
In Silence pass, so friendly to thy Lays.

     Hark! how the Birds, on ev'ry blooming Spray,
With spritely Notes accuse thy dull Delay:
See how the Spring, adorn'd with gaudy Pride
10 And youthful Beauty, smiles on ev'ry Side!
Here painted Flow'rs in gay Confusion grow;
There chrystal Streams in wild *Meanders* flow:
The sprouting Trees their leafy Honours wear,
And *Zephyrs* whisper thro' the balmy Air.
15 All things to Verse invite. But, O! my Muse,
What lofty Theme, what Subject wilt thou chuse?
The Praise of Wine let Vulgar Bards indite,

And Love's soft Joys in wanton Strains recite;
With Nobler Thoughts do Thou my Soul inspire,
20   And with Diviner Warmth my Bosom fire.

    Thee, *BEST* and *GREATEST!* let my grateful Lays,
Parent of Universal Nature, praise!
All things are full of Thee! Where-e'er mine Eye
Is turn'd, I still thy present Godhead spy!
25   Each Herb the Footsteps of thy Wisdom bears,
And ev'ry Blade of Grass thy Pow'r declares!
As yon' clear Lake the pendent Image shows
Of ev'ry Flow'r that on its Border grows;
So, in the fair Creation's Glass, we find
30   A faint Reflection of th' Eternal Mind.

    Whate'er of Goodness and of Excellence
In Nature's various Scene accost the Sense,
To Thee alone their whole Perfection owe,
From Thee, as from their proper Fountain, flow.

35   Fair are the Stars, that grace the sable Night,
And Beauteous is the Dawn of Rosie Light;
Lovely the Prospect, that each flow'ry Field,
These limpid Streams and shady Forests yield:
To Thee compar'd, nor Fair the Stars of Night,
40   Nor Beauteous is the Dawn of Rosie Light;
Nor Lovely is the Scene, each flow'ry Field,
The limpid Streams and shady Forests yield.

    Incapable of Bounds, above all Height,
Thou art invisible to Mortal Sight;
45   Thy-self thy Palace! And, sustain'd by Thee,
All live and move in thy Immensity.
Thy Voice Omnipotent did Infant-Day
Thro' the dark Realms of empty Space display,
This glorious Arch of heav'nly *Sapphire* rear,
50   And spread this Canopy of liquid Air.

133

At Thy Command, the Starry Host, the Sun,
And Moon, unerringly their Courses run;
Ceaseless they move, Obsequious to fullfil
The Task assign'd by Thy Almighty Will.
55   Thy Vital Pow'r, diffus'd from Pole to Pole,
Inspires and animates this ample Whole.

If Thou wert Absent, the Material Mass
Wou'd without Motion lie in boundless Space.
The Sun, arrested in his Spiral Way,
60   No longer wou'd dispense alternate Day;
A breathless Calm wou'd hush the stormy Wind,
And a new Frost the flowing Rivers bind.

Whate'er, thro' false Philosophy, is thought
To be by *Chance* or *Parent-Nature* wrought,
65   From Thee alone proceeds. With timely Rain
Thou sate'st the thirsty Field and springing Grain.
Inspir'd by Thee, the *Northern* Tempests sweep
The bending Corn, and toss the foamy Deep:
Inspir'd by Thee, the softer *Southern* Breeze
70   Wafts fragrant Odours thro' the trembling Trees.
By Thee conducted thro' the darksom Caves
And Veins of hollow Earth, the briny Waves
In bubling Springs and fruitful Fountains rise,
And spout their sweeten'd Streams against the Skies.

75   By Thee, the Brutal Kind are taught to chuse
Their proper Good, and Noxious things refuse;
Hence each conforms his Actions to his Place,
Knows to preserve his Life, and propagate his Race.
Hence the wise Conduct of the painful Bee;
80   Who future Want does constantly foresee,
Contrive her waxen Cells with curious Skill,
And with rich Stores of gather'd Honey fill.
Hence the gay Birds, that sport in fluid Air,
Soft Nests, to lodge their callow Young, prepare,

85 Rear with unweari'd Toil the tender Brood,
   From Harms protect, and furnish 'em with Food.

      But Man, whom thy peculiar Grace design'd
   The Image of thine own Eternal Mind,
   Man thy chief Favourite, Thou did'st inspire
90 With a bright Spark of thy Celestial Fire.
   Rich with a Thinking Soul, with piercing Eye
   He views the spacious Earth and distant Sky;
   And sees the various Marks of Skill Divine,
   That in each Part of Nature's System shine.
95 Him therefore it becomes, in grateful Lays,
   To sing his bounteous Maker's solemn Praise.

TEXTUAL SOURCES

Addison, Joseph, "An Ode". *The Spectator,* ed. D. F. Bond (Oxford, 1965), IV, 144-5.

Carey, Henry, "The Ballad of Sally in our Alley". *Early Eighteenth Century Poetry,* ed. J. Sutherland (London, 1965), pp. 184-5.

Congreve, William, *The Complete Works,* ed. M. Summers (New York, 1924).
"A Hue and Cry after Fair Amoret", IV, 74;
"Song" ('Cruel Amynta . . . '), IV, 77;
"Song" ('Pious Selinda . . . '), IV, 78.

Defoe, Daniel, "The True-born Englishman. A Satyr" ('Introduction'). *The Novels and Selected Writings* (Oxford, 1927-8), I, 31-2.

Gay John, *The Poetical Works,* ed. G. C. Faber (London, 1926).
"A Ballad", pp. 357-8;
"Newgate's Garland", pp. 186-8;
"Saturday or The Flights", pp. 51-4;
"Sweet William's Farewell to Black-ey'd Susan", pp. 181-3.

Johnson, Samuel, "London". *The Yale Edition of the Works.* Vol. IV: *Poems,* ed. E. L. McAdam, Jr., with G. Milne (New Haven, 1964), pp. 47-61.

Needler, Henry, "A Vernal Hymn, in Praise of the Creator". *The Works of Mr. Henry Needler (1728),* Publ. of the Aug. Repr. Soc. (Los Angeles, 1961), pp. 63-8.

"A New Song entitled the Warming Pan". *The Common Muse,* ed. V. de Sola Pinto and A. E. Rodway (London, 1957), pp. 82-3.

Parnell, Thomas, "Song". *The Twickenham Edition of the Poems of Alexander Pope.* Vol. VI: *Minor Poems,* ed. N. Ault and John Butt (London, 1954), p. 436.

Pope Alexander, *The Twickenham Edition* (Oxford, 1939-67).
"Epitaph on Charles Earl of Dorset", VI, 334-5;
"Epitaph on Sir William Trumbull", VI, 169;
"An Essay on Criticism" (Part i), vol. I *(Pastoral Poetry and An Essay on Criticism,* ed. E. Audra and A. Williams, 1961), pp. 229-63;
"The First Satire of the Second Book of Horace Imitated", vol. IV *(Imitations of Horace,* ed. John Butt, [2]1953), pp. 5-21;
"Fragment of a Satire", VI, 283-5;
"The Rape of the Lock", vol. II *(The Rape of the Lock,* ed. G. Tillotson, [2]1954), pp. 144-206;
"Spring", I, 59-70.

Prior, Matthew, *The Literary Works,* ed. H. B. Wright and M. K. Spears (Oxford, 1959).

"A Better Answer", I, 450-1;

"Jinny the Just", I, 300-4;

" 'Since we your husband daily see' ", I, 711;

"To Phillis", I, 702-3.

Savage, Richard, "Epitaph on a young Lady". *The Poetical Works,* ed. C. Tracy (Cambridge, 1962), pp. 159-60.

Swift, Jonathan, *The Poems,* ed. H. Williams (Oxford, 1937).

"The Beasts Confession to the Priest", II, 601-8;

"A Description of a City Shower", I, 136-9;

"On Poetry: A Rapsody", II, 640-57;

"A Satirical Elegy on the Death of a Late Famous General", I, 295-7;

"Strephon and Chloe", II, 584-93.

Thomson, James, *The Complete Poetical Works,* ed. J. L. Robertson (London, 1908).

"To the Memory of Sir Isaac Newton", pp. 436-42;

"Winter. A Poem", pp. 228-38.

Tickell, Thomas, "Colin and Lucy". *The Literary Ballad,* ed. A. H. Ehrenpreis, Arnold's English Texts (London, 1966), pp. 28-30.

"The Vicar of Bray". *The Oxford Book of Light Verse,* ed. W. H. Auden (Oxford, 1938), pp. 260-2.

Watts, Isaac, "A Cradle Hymn". *The Oxford Book of English Verse,* ed. A. Quiller-Couch (Oxford, 1900), pp. 499-500;

"Hymn". *Isaac Watts. Hymns and Spiritual Songs 1707-1748,* ed. S. L. Bishop (London, 1962), pp. 208-9.

Winchilsea, Anne Countess of, *The Poems,* ed. Myra Reynolds, Decennial Publications of the University of Chicago, 2nd ser. 5 (Chicago, 1903).

"A Song", p. 129.

BIBLIOGRAPHY

I. Anthologies

The Works of the English Poets. From Chaucer to Cowper, ed. A. Chalmers, with Prefaces, Biographical and Critical, by Samuel Johnson, 21 vols. London, 1810.

English and Scottish Popular Ballads, ed. F. J. Child, 5 vols. Boston and New York, 1882-98.

Forgotten Lyrics of the Eighteenth Century, ed. O. Doughty. London, 1924.

The Oxford Book of Eighteenth Century Verse, ed. D. Nichol Smith. Oxford, 1926.

Poems on Several Occasions, Written in the Eighteenth Century, ed. K. W. Campbell [Percy Reprints, IX.]. Oxford, 1926.

Minor Poets of the Eighteenth Century, ed. H. I. A. Fausset. [Everyman's Library.] London, 1930.

Georgian Satirists, ed. S. Vines. London, 1934.

The Common Muse. An Anthology of Popular British Ballad Poetry, XVth-XXth Century, ed. V. de Sola Pinto and A. E. Rodway. London, 1957.

Early Eighteenth Century Poetry, ed. J. Sutherland. Arnold's English Texts. London, 1965.

II. Individual Authors (Editions)

Addison, Joseph:
The Miscellaneous Works, 2 vols, ed. A. C. Guthkelch. London, 1914.
Occasional Verses, ed. R. Blanchard. Oxford, 1952.

Carey, Henry:
Songs and Poems, ed. M. Gibbings. London, 1924.
The Poems, ed. F. T. Wood. London, 1930.

Congreve, William:
The Complete Works, 4 vols, ed. M. Summers. New York, 1924.
The Mourning Bride and other Works, ed. B. Dobrée. [World's Classics.] Oxford, 1928.
The Works, ed. F. W. Bateson. London, 1930.

Defoe, Daniel:
Novels and Selected Writings, 14 vols. Oxford, 1927-8.

Gay, John:
The Poetical Works, ed. G. C. Faber. London, 1926.
Selected Poems, ed. A. Ross. London, 1950.

Johnson, Samuel:
The Poems, ed. D. Nichol Smith and E. L. McAdam. Oxford, 1941.
The Yale Edition of the Works. Vol. IV: *Poems,* ed. E. L. McAdam, Jr., with G. Milne. New Haven, 1964.

Parnell, Thomas:
Minor Poets of the Eighteenth Century, ed. H. I. A. Fausset. [Everyman's Library.] London, 1930.

Pope, Alexander:
The Twickenham Edition, 10 vols, gen. ed. J. Butt. Oxford, 1939-67.
Vol. I: *Pastoral Poetry and An Essay on Criticism,* ed. E. Audra and A. Williams. 1961.
Vol. II: *The Rape of the Lock and other Poems,* ed. G. Tillotson. 1940; 1954 (rev. edn.).
Vol. III, i: *An Essay on Man,* ed. M. Mack. 1950.
Vol. III, ii: *Epistles to Several Persons (Moral Essays),* ed. F. W. Bateson. 1951.
Vol. IV: *Imitations of Horace,* ed. J. Butt. 1939; 1953 (rev. edn.).
Vol. V: *The Dunciad,* ed. J. R. Sutherland. 1943; 1953 (rev. edn.).
Vol. VI: *Minor Poems,* ed. N. Ault and J. Butt. 1954.

Prior, Matthew:
Writings, 2 vols., ed. A. R. Waller. Cambridge, 1905-7.
The Literary Works, 2 vols., ed. H. B. Wright and M. K. Spears. Oxford, 1959.

Savage, Richard:
The Poetical Works, ed. C. Tracy. Cambridge, 1962.

Swift, Jonathan:
The Poems, 3 vols., ed. H. Williams. Oxford, 1937.
Collected Poems, 2 vols., ed. J. Horrell. [Muses' Library.] London, 1958.

Thomson, James:
The Seasons (vol. I); *The Castle of Indolence and other Poems* (vol. II), ed.
H. D. Roberts and Sir E. Gosse. [Muses' Library.] London, 1906.
The Complete Poetical Works, ed. J. L. Robertson. London, 1908.

Watts, Isaac:
Hymns and Spiritual Songs 1707-1748, ed. S. L. Bishop. London, 1962.

Winchilsea, Anne Countess of:
The Poems, ed. Myra Reynolds. [Decennial Publications of the University
of Chicago, Second Series V.] Chicago, 1903.

Young, Edward:
The Poetical Works, 2 vols., ed. J. Mitford. London, 1830.

III. The Social and Cultural Context

a) Politics and Social Life

W. E. Mead, *The Grand Tour in the Eighteenth Century.* Boston, 1914.
A. S. Turberville, *English Men and Manners in the Eighteenth Century.* Ox-
ford, 1926.
W. T. Lamprade, *Public Opinion and Politics in Eighteenth-Century Eng-
land.* New York, 1936.
G. N. Clark, *Science and Social Welfare in the Age of Newton.* Oxford,
1937.
B. Williams, *The Whig Supremacy, 1714-1760.* Oxford, 1939; rev. edn.
1962.
J. H. Plumb, *England in the Eighteenth Century.* [Pelican Books.] Har-
mondsworth, 1950; rev. edn. 1963.
G. M. Trevelyan, *Illustrated English Social History.* Vols. II and III. [Pelican
Books.] Harmondsworth, 1950-55.
G. E. Mingay, *English Landed Society in the Eighteenth Century,* London
and Toronto, 1963.

b) Religion, Philosophy, Science, Arts

L. Stephen, *History of English Thought in the Eighteenth Century,* 2 vols.
London, 1876-80.
J. B. Bury, *The Idea of Progress.* London, 1920.
H. J. Laski, *Political Thought in England: Locke to Bentham.* London,
1920.
B. Willey, *The Eighteenth Century Background.* London, 1940.

R. A. Knox, *Enthusiasm. A Chapter in the History of Religion.* Oxford, 1950.

E. Cassirer, *The Philosophy of the Enlightenment.* Princeton, 1951.

A. Wolf, *A History of Science, Technology, and Philosophy in the Eighteenth Century.* Rev. McKie, London, 1952.

E. K. Waterhouse, *Painting in Britain, 1530-1790.* [Pelican Books.] Harmondsworth, 1953.

G. R. Cragg, *The Church and the Age of Reason, 1648-1789.* [Pelican Books.] Harmondsworth, 1960.

G. R. Cragg, *Authority and Reason in the Eighteenth Century.* Cambridge, 1964.

D. Irwin, *English Neoclassical Art. Studies in Inspiration and Taste.* Greenwich, Conn., 1965.

IV. Augustan Poetry (General Studies)

a) Surveys

W. J. Courthope, *A History of English Poetry.* Vol. III. London, 1903.

O. Elton, *A Survey of English Literature, 1730-1780,* 2 vols. London, 1928.

J. R. Sutherland, *A Preface to Eighteenth Century Poetry.* Oxford, 1948.

G. Sherburne and D. F. Bond, "The Restoration and Eighteenth Century, 1660-1789". In *A Literary History of England,* ed. A. C. Baugh. 2nd revd. edn., New York, 1967.

J. Butt, *The Augustan Age.* London, 1950.

B. Ford (ed.), *The Pelican Guide to English Literature.* Vol. IV: *From Dryden to Johnson.* Harmondsworth, 1957; revd. edn. 1968.

B. Dobrée, *English Literature in the Early Eighteenth Century, 1700-1740. Oxford History of English Literature,* vol. VII. Oxford, 1959.

J. Clifford, "The Eighteenth Century", *Modern Language Quarterly,* 26 (1965), 111-134.

R. H. Paulson, "Recent Studies in the Restoration and Eighteenth Century", *Studies in English Literature 1500-1900,* 7 (1967), 531-58.

b) The "Augustan Mode"

J. L. Lowes, *Convention and Revolt in Poetry.* Boston, 1919.

F. Gallaway, *Rule, Reason, and Revolt in English Classicism.* New York, 1940.

W. K. Wimsatt, Jr., "The Augustan Mode in English Poetry", *English Literary History,* 20 (1953), 1-14.

B. Bronson, "The Pre-Romantic or Post-Augustan Mode", *English Literary History,* 20 (1953), 15-28.

B. Bronson, "When was Neo-Classicism?". *Studies in Criticism and Aesthetics, 1660-1800. Essays in Honour of Samuel Holt Monk,* ed. H. Anderson and J. S. Shea (Minneapolis, 1967), pp. 13-35.

R. Cohen, "The Augustan Mode in English Poetry", *Eighteenth Century Studies,* 1 (1967), 3-32.

c) Poetry and Society

A. Beljame, *Men of Letters and the English Public, 1660-1744.* Paris, 1881; ed. B. Dobrée, London, 1948.

L. Stephen, *English Literature and Society in the Eighteenth Century.* London, 1904.

C. B. Tinker, *The Salon and English Letters.* New York, 1915.

V. Lange, *Die Lyrik und ihr Publikum im England des 18. Jahrhunderts. Eine geschmacksgeschichtliche Untersuchung über die englischen Anthologien von 1670-1780.* Weimar, 1935.

A. R. Humphreys, *The Augustan World. Life and Letters in Eighteenth-Century England.* London, 1954.

G. Stratmann, *Englische Aristokratie und klassizistische Dichtung. Eine literatursoziologische Studie.* [Erlanger Beiträge zur Sprach- und Kunstwissenschaft.] Nürnberg, 1965.

V. Augustan Poetry – Literary and Intellectual Influences

a) Literary Influences

C. M. Goad, *Horace in the English Literature of the Eighteenth Century.* New Haven, 1918.

E. Nitchie, *Vergil and the English Poets.* New York, 1919.

A. F. B. Clark, *Boileau and the French Classical Critics in England (1660-1830).* [Bibliothèque de la Révue de Littérature Comparée.] Paris, 1925.

P. S. Wood, "Native Elements in English Neo-Classicism", *Modern Philology,* 24 (1926), 201-8.

E. R. Wasserman, *Elizabethan Poetry in the Eighteenth Century.* Urbana, 1949.

W. J. Bate, "The English Poet and the Burden of the Past, 1660-1820". In *Aspects of the Eighteenth Century,* ed. E. R. Wasserman. Baltimore, 1965.

b) Religion, Philosophy, Science

A. O. Love;oy, "The Parallel of Deism and Classicism", *Modern Philology,* 29 (1932), 281-299.

K. MacLean, *John Locke and English Literature of the Eighteenth Century.* New Haven, 1936.

H. N. Fairchild, *Religious Trends in English Poetry, 1700-1780,* 2 vols. New York, 1939-42.

M. H. Nicolson, *Newton Demands the Muse.* Princeton, 1946.

J. Butt, "Science and Man in Eighteenth-Century Poetry", *Durham University Journal,* 39 (1947), 79-88.

D. Bush, *Science and English Poetry.* New York, 1950.

B. Dobrée, *The Broken Cistern.* London, 1954.

J. H. Hagstrum, *The Sister Arts. The Tradition of Literary Pictorialism and English Poetry: From Dryden to Gray.* Chicago, 1958.

I. Kovacevich, "The Mechanical Muse: The Impact of Technical Inventions on Eighteenth-Century Neo-Classical Poetry", *Huntingdon Library Quarterly,* 28 (1965), 263-81.

E. Wolff, *Shaftesbury und seine Bedeutung für die englische Literatur des 18. Jahrhunderts: der Moralist und die literarische Form.* Tübingen 1960.

VI. Augustan Poetry – Themes and Literary Forms

a) Critical Theory

A. O. Lovejoy, "'Nature' as Aesthetic Norm", *Modern Language Notes,* 42 (1927), 444-50.

S. H. Monk, *The Sublime: A Study of Critical Theories in XVIII – Century England.* New York, 1935.

D. F. Bond, "The Neo-Classical Psychology of the Imagination", *English Literary History,* 4 (1937), 245-64.

R. F. Jones, *Ancients and Moderns: A Study of the Background of the Battle of the Books.* St. Louis, 1936.

J. H. W. Atkins, *English Literary Criticism: Seventeenth and Eighteenth-Centuries.* London, 1951.

E. R. Marks, *Relativist and Absolutist: The Early Neoclassical Debate in England.* New Brunswick, N. J., 1955.

S. Elledge (ed.), *Eighteenth Century Critical Essays,* 2 vols. Ithaca, 1961.

R. Marsh, *Four Dialectical Theories of Poetry: An Aspect of English Neo-Classical Criticism.* Chicago, 1965.

b) Themes

M. Reynolds, *The Treatment of Nature in English Poetry between Pope and Wordsworth.* Chicago, 1896.

C. E. de Haas, *Nature and the Country in English Poetry of the First Half of the Eighteenth Century.* Amsterdam, 1928.

A. O. Lovejoy, *The Great Chain of Being.* Cambridge, Mass., 1936.

M. M. Fitzgerald, *First Follow Nature. Primitivism in English Poetry, 1725-1750.* New York, 1947.

B. Dobrée, *The Theme of Patriotism in the Poetry of the Early Eighteenth Century.* [Warton Lectures on British Poetry.] London, 1949.

M.-S. Røstvig, *The Happy Man,* 2 vols. [Oslo Studies in English.] Oslo, 1954-1958.

P. Fussell, *The Rhetorical World of Augustan Humanism: Ethics and Imagery from Swift to Burke.* Oxford, 1965.

c) Verse and Style

W. C. Brown, *The Triumph of Form. A Study of the Later Masters of the Heroic Couplet.* Chapel Hill, 1948.

D. Davie, *Purity of Diction in English Verse.* London, 1952.

D. Greene, "'Logical Structure' in Eighteenth-Century Poetry", *Philological Quarterly,* 31 (1952), 315-36.

D. Davie, *Articulate Energy: An Inquiry into the Syntax of English Poetry.* London, 1955.

B. Groom, *The Diction of Poetry from Spenser to Bridges.* Toronto, 1955.

C. F. Chapin, *Personification in Eighteenth-Century English Poetry.* New York, 1955.

R. Trickett, *The Honest Muse. A Study in Augustan Verse.* Oxford, 1967.

K.-H. Göller, "Die *Poetic Diction* des 18. Jahrhunderts in England", *Deutsche Vierteljahresschrift für Literaturwissenschaft und Geistesgeschichte,* 33 (1964), 24-39.

d) Pastoral and Georgic Traditions

M. H. Shackford, "A Definition of the Pastoral Idyll", *Publ. of the Modern Language Association,* 19 (1904), 583-92.

R. T. Kerlin, *Theocritus in English Literature.* Lynchberg, Virg., 1910.

M. L. Lilly, *The Georgic.* Baltimore, 1919.

R. F. Jones, "Eclogue Types in English Poetry of the Eighteenth Century", *Journal of English and Germanic Philology,* 24 (1925), 33-60.

M. K. Bragg, *The Formal Eclogue in Eighteenth-Century England.* [Maine University Studies.] Orono, 1926.

D. L. Durling, *Georgic Tradition in English Poetry.* New York, 1935.

W. Empson, *Some Versions of Pastoral.* New York, 1938.

J. E. Congleton, *Theories of Pastoral in England,* 1648-1798. Gainesville, 1952.

D. S. McCoy, *Tradition and Convention: A Study of Periphrasis in English Pastoral Poetry from 1557-1715.* The Hague, 1965.

e) The Heroic Tradition

F. Brie, *Englische Rokoko-Epik (1710-1730).* Munich, 1927.

H. T. Swedenberg, Jr., *The Theory of the Epic in England, 1650-1800.* Berkeley, Calif., 1944.

E. M. W. Tillyard, *The English Epic and Its Background.* London, 1954.

R. Sühnel, *Homer und die englische Humanität.* Tübingen, 1958.

U. Broich, *Studien zum komischen Epos. Ein Beitrag zur Deutung, Typologie und Geschichte des komischen Epos im englischen Klassizismus.* Tübingen, 1968.

f) The Satire

C. W. Previté-Orton, *Political Satire in English Poetry.* Cambridge, 1910.

H. Walker, *English Satire and Satirists.* London and New York, 1925.

D. Worcester, *The Art of Satire.* Cambridge, Mass., 1940.

M. C. Randolph, "The Structural Design of the Formal Satire", *Philological Quarterly,* 21 (1942), 368-84.

I. Jack, *Augustan Satire. Intent and Idiom in English Poetry, 1660-1750.* Oxford, 1952.

J. Sutherland, *English Satire.* Cambridge, 1958.

R. C. Elliott, *The Power of Satire.* Princeton, 1960.

A. B. Kernan, *The Plot of Satire.* New Haven, 1965.

H. D. Weinbrot, "The Pattern of Formal Verse Satire in the Restoration and the Eighteenth Century", *Publ. of the Modern Language Association,* 80 (1965), 394-401.

B. A. Goldgar, "Satires on Man and 'The Dignity of Human Nature'", *Publ. of the Modern Language Association,* 80 (1965), 535-41.

g) Other Forms of Poetry

S. B. Hustvedt, *Ballad Criticism during the Eighteenth Century.* Cambridge, Mass., 1916.

O. Doughty, *The English Lyric in the Age of Reason.* London, 1922.

G. N. Shuster, *The English Ode from Milton to Keats.* New York, 1924.

O. Doughty, "Eighteenth Century Song", *English Studies,* 7 (1925), 161-69.

C. A. Moore, "Whig Panegyric Verse 1700-1760: A Phase of Sentimentalism", *Publ. of the Modern Language Association,* 41 (1926), 362-401.

R. P. Bond, *English Burlesque Poetry 1700-1750.* [Harvard Studies in English.] Cambridge, 1932.

C. W. Peltz, "The Neo-Classic Lyric, 1660-1725", *English Literary History,* 9 (1944), 92-116.

N. Maclean, "From Action to Image: Theories of the Lyric in the Eighteenth Century". In *Critics and Criticism,* Chicago, 1952.

B. Friedman, *The Ballad Revival.* Chicago, 1961.

K. Schlüter, *Die englische Ode.* Bonn, 1964.

W. Franke, *Gattungskonstanten des englischen Versepitaphs von Ben Jonson zu Alexander Pope.* Diss. Erlangen, 1964.

H. D. Weinbrot, "Translation and Parody: Towards the Genealogy of the Augustan Imitation", *English Literary History,* 33 (1967), 434-47.

VII. Individual Poets (Studies)

Carey, Henry:

W. H. Hudson, *A Quiet Cormer in a Library.* London, 1915.

R. G. Noyes, "The Contemporary Reception of *Sally in our Alley",* *Harvard Studies and Notes in Philology and Literature,* 18 (1935), 165-76.

Defoe, Daniel:

A. C. Guthkelch, "Defoe's *True-born Englishman",* *Essays and Studies,* 4 (1913), 27-42.

Shinagel, M., *Daniel Defoe and Middle-Class Gentility.* Cambridge, Mass., 1968.

Gay, John:

W. H. Irving, *Gay, Favorite of the Wits.* Durham, N. C., 1940.

W. C. Brown, "Gay's Mastery of the Heroic Couplet", *Publ. of the Modern Language Association,* 61 (1946), 114-25.

H. Trowbridge, "Pope, Gay, and *The Shepherd's Week",* *Modern Language Quarterly,* 5 (1944), 79-88.

J. Sutherland, "Gay". In *Pope and His Contemporaries. Essays Presented to George Sherburne.* Oxford, 1949.

S. M. Armens, *John Gay, Social Critic.* New York, 1954.

J. M. Aden, "The 1720 Version of *Rural Sports* and the Georgic Tradition", *Modern Language Quarterly,* 20 (1944), 228-32.

A. Forsgren, *John Gay, Poet 'of a Lower Order'. Comments on his Rural Poems and Other Early Writings.* Stockholm, 1964.

C. B. Teske, "Gay's 'Twas When the Seas Were Roaring' and the Rise of Pathetic Balladry", *Anglia,* 83 (1965), 411-25.

Johnson, Samuel:
F. R. Leavis, "Johnson and Augustanism" and "Johnson as Poet". In *The Common Pursuit.* London, 1952.
J. L. Clifford, *Young Sam Johnson.* New York, 1955.

Pope, Alexander:
A. Warren, *Pope as a Critic and Humanist.* Princeton, 1929.
R. K. Root, *The Poetical Career of Pope.* Princeton, 1938.
A. E. Case, "Pope, Addison, and the Atticus Lines", *Modern Philology,* 33 (1935), 187-93.
N. Ault, *New Light on Pope.* London, 1949.
R. P. Parkin, *The Poetic Workmanship of Alexander Pope.* Minneapolis, 1955.
G. Tillotson, *Pope and Human Nature.* Oxford, 1958.
R. W. Rogers, *The Major Satires of Alexander Pope.* Urbana, 1955.
R. A. Brower, *Alexander Pope: The Poetry of Allusion.* Oxford, 1959.
B. Boyce, *The Character Sketches in Pope's Poems.* Durham, 1962.
A. Williams, "The 'Fall' of China and *The Rape of the Lock*", *Philological Quarterly,* 13 (1962), 412-25.
T. E. Maresca, "Pope's Defense of Satire: *The First Satire of the Second Book of Horace, Imitated*", *English Literary History,* 31 (1964), 336-94.
T. E. Maresca, *Pope's Horatian Poems.* Columbus, 1966.

Prior, Matthew:
O. Doughty, "The Poet of the 'Familiar Style'", English Studies, 7 (1925), 5-10.
C. K. Eves, *Matthew Prior: Poet and Diplomatist.* New York, 1939.
M. K. Spears, "Some Ethical Aspects of Matthew Prior's Poetry", *Studies in Philology,* 45 (1948), 606-629.
G. Stratmann, "Matthew Prior: 'To Phillis'". In *Die Englische Lyrik,* 2 vols., ed. K.-H. Göller (Düsseldorf, 1968). Vol. I, 211-220.

Savage, Richard:
C. Tracy, *The Artificial Bastard: A Biography of Richard Savage.* Toronto, 1953.

Swift, Jonathan:
F. Ball, *Swift's Verse: An Essay.* London, 1929.
R. Quintana, *Swift. An Introduction.* London, 1955.
E. W. Rosenheim, *Swift and the Satirist's Art.* Chicago, 1963.

M. Voigt, *Swift and the Twentieth Century.* Detroit, 1964.

H. D. Davis, *Jonathan Swift: Essays on His Satire and Other Studies.* New York, 1964.

D. Greene, "On Swift's 'Scatological' Poems", *Sewanee Review,* 75 (1967), 672-89.

Thomson, James:

R. D. Havens, "Primitivism and the Idea of Progress in Thomson", *Studies in Philology,* 29 (1932), 41-52.

H. Drennon, "Scientific Rationalism and James Thomson's Poetic Art", *Studies in Philology,* 31 (1934), 453-71.

A. D. McKillop, *The Background of Thomson's 'Seasons'.* Minneapolis, 1942.

D. Grant, *James Thomson, Poet of "The Seasons".* London, 1951.

P. M. Spacks, *The Varied God: A Critical Study of Thomson's 'Seasons'.* Berkeley, 1959.

J. Chalker, "Thomson's *Seasons* and Virgil's *Georgics*", *Studia Neophil.,* 35 (1963), 41-56.

R. Cohen, *The Art of Discrimination. Thomson's 'The Seasons' and the Language of Criticism.* Berkeley, 1964.

Tickell, Thomas:

R. E. Tickell, *Thomas Tickell and the Eighteenth Century Poets (1685-1740).* London, 1931.

Watts, Isaac:

V. de Sola Pinto, "Isaac Watts and the Adventurous Muse", *Essays and Studies,* 20 (1935), 86-107.

H. Escott, *Isaac Watts, Hymnographer: A Study of the Beginnings, Development, and Philosophy of the English Hymn.* London, 1962.

Winchilsea, Anne Countess of:

R. A. Brower, "Lady Winchilsea and the Poetic Tradition of the Seventeenth Century", *Studies in Philology,* 46 (1945), 30-38.